Florida A&M University, Tallahassee
Florida Atlantic University, Boca Raton
Florida Gulf Coast University, Ft. Myers
Florida International University, Miami
Florida State University, Tallahassee
University of Central Florida, Orlando
University of Florida, Gainesville
University of North Florida, Jacksonville
University of South Florida, Tampa
University of West Florida, Pensacola

Iyá (2001) by Alexis Esquivel "A Mariana, a mi Madre, y por supuesto a Excilia que es igual" [To Mariana, to my Mother, and of course, to Excilia, who is the same].

The 28" x 41" canvas depicts the figure of Mariana Grajales, the mother of Afro-Cuban independence fighter General Antonio Maceo, playing the lead batá drum known as Iyá, or the Mother Drum. Mariana Grajales stands as a symbol of motherhood as well as of Afro-Cuban pride. This painting acts as homage to Cuban artist Belkis Ayón (1968–1999), who produced large-scale engravings based on myths derived from the all-male Abakuá secret society in Cuba. Excilia Saldaña, in conversation with the translators, said that the figure of her grandmother, Ana Excilia Bregante, so central to her poetry, also represents the figure of Mariana Grajales. Photograph by Donald Gurewitz.

In the Vortex of the Cyclone

Selected Poems by Excilia Saldaña

A Bilingual Edition

Edited and Translated by Flora M. González Mandri
and Rosamond Rosenmeier

University Press of Florida
Gainesville · Tallahassee · Tampa · Boca Raton
Pensacola · Orlando · Miami · Jacksonville · Ft. Myers

Copyright 2002 by Flora M. González Mandri and Rosamond Rosenmeier
Printed in the United States of America on acid-free, TCF (totally chlorine-free) paper
All rights reserved

07 06 05 04 03 02   6 5 4 3 2 1

Cataloging-in-publication data are available from the Library of Congress.
ISBN 0-8130-2459-5

The University Press of Florida is the scholarly publishing agency for the State
University System of Florida, comprising Florida A&M University, Florida Atlantic
University, Florida Gulf Coast University, Florida International University, Florida
State University, University of Central Florida, University of Florida, University
of North Florida, University of South Florida, and University of West Florida.

University Press of Florida
15 Northwest 15th Street
Gainesville, FL 32611-2079
http://www.upf.com

To
Excilia Saldaña, In Memoriam,
and
Mario Ernesto Romero, her
"Child-Cosmos"

Flora Mandri, In Memoriam,
and
Rachel, Jeremy, Flora and Samuel,
Sean,
Laura,
Rob and Gail

Evelyn Rauch, In Memoriam,
and Jason, Susan, and Jackson,
Twyla, Manuel, Rachel, Malcolm and Emily,
Alan and Louisa,
Peter and Leah

En el vórtice del ciclón
sólo se admite al que tenga vocación de ventolera.

In the vortex of the cyclone
only those with a vocation for gusts of wind are admitted.

Contents

Prólogo

A Gerardo Fulleda León, por quien la conocí.
A Esteban Llorach, que vela y guarda su memoria.
A Mayito

Pocas veces un ciclón asoma sus fauces de una forma tan clara y definida. Habitualmente, los ciclones nacen de un azar pero su nacimiento y su tiempo de organización pueden alcanzar días y hasta semanas, o fracciones de segundos. Los habitantes de las islas toman sus precauciones pero, en la mayoría de los casos, ninguno puede adivinar ni su paradero ni su destino. Si algo se sabe, con certeza, es que el ciclón, si amenaza con ser demasiado perturbador—como es usual también—tendrá nombre de mujer.

El ciclón que colocó a Excilia Saldaña en la cumbre de la expresión literaria cubana lleva su propio nombre, derivado del de su abuela materna Ana Excilia Bregante y sus primeras lluvias huracanadas se nombraron "Ofumelli,"[1] palabra mágica de esa babel en ruinas que componen las lenguas traídas por los esclavos trasplantados al Nuevo Mundo desde las costas occidentales de África.

El misterio encerrado en este vocablo dejó boquiabiertos a los miembros del Jurado del Premio Casa de las Américas instalado en La Habana de 1967. Se trataba de un largo poema cuyo aliento personalísimo integraba un poemario aún mayor, *Enlloró*[2] que, tiempo después, disfrutaría de la preferencia de lectores recién alfabetizados y de una vanguardia interesada en cultivar no sólo una estética fundamentalmente comunicativa sino que añoraba restaurar en su justo sitio a esa vasta tradición oral que provenía de la cultura cubana más viva y cambiante.

Ya para entonces Excilia había elegido estrenar sus lanzas bebiendo de nuestras fuentes de antecedente africano y asimilando las lecciones de los juglares del Medioevo español. Así llegó a nosotros, con voz juglaresca y

Foreword

To Gerardo Fulleda León, through whom I met her.
To Esteban Llorach, who keeps and watches over her memory.
To Mayito.

Seldom does a cyclone show its throat in a form so clear and defined. Usually, cyclones come about by chance, but their birth and time of development can take days and even weeks, or fragments of seconds. The inhabitants of the islands take precautions, but, in the majority of cases, no one can guess either the cyclone's whereabouts or its destiny. If there is anything that may be known with certainty, it is that the cyclone, if it threatens much disruption—as is often the case—it will bear the name of a woman.

The cyclone that placed Excilia Saldaña at the summit of Cuban literary expression bears her own name, derived from that of her maternal grandmother Ana Excilia Bregante; and its first hurricane rains were called "Ofumelli,"[1] the magic word from that ruined Babel constituted by the languages brought by the slaves uprooted to the New World from the western coast of Africa.

The mystery enclosed in this word "Ofumelli" baffled the members of the jury of the Casa de las Américas Prize, assembled in Havana in 1967. It was all about a long poem whose intensely personal breath was part of a greater poetic anthology, *Enlloró*,[2] which not much later would enjoy the preference of recently literate readers and of a cultural vanguard interested in cultivating not only a fundamentally communicative aesthetic, but also the return to its just place of that vast oral tradition that came from the most vibrant and dynamic Cuban cultural source.

Even then, Excilia had chosen to introduce her spears, drinking from the source of our African antecedents and assimilating the lessons of the troubadours of the Spanish Medieval. Thus, she came to us, with a

ese acento negro que había inaugurado en nuestra poesía Nicolás Guillén desde el 20 de abril de 1930. Desde siempre, el vórtice de su ciclón la hizo moverse entre el cultivo de nanas preciosas—de una gracia formal realmente envidiable—y ese verso libre, como de epopeya tropical, que le sirve para trazar el mapa de todo un archipiélago de valores civiles, morales, históricos. Tal pareciera que un pájaro azul, un ave de plumaje elegíaco, ha sobrevolado el mapa de su Isla, salvándose de tanto desgarramiento humano, de tanta angustia familiar, de tanto sentimiento filial en busca de un país más justo y más liberador.

Excilia Saldaña logró encontrar la voz histórica de la mujer cubana buscando su origen en los barcos negreros, en esa amarga travesía que data del siglo XVI y que subió a las montañas durante las dos guerras necesarias del siglo XIX. Buscó por fuera una herencia de opresión y la puso ante el espejo para revelarnos cuan endeudados estamos todos con ese pasado de despojo y depredación nacido en las plantaciones no sólo cubanas sino de todo el Caribe y de las Américas negras.

Danzón macabro el suyo, bailado por abuelas y esposas de todos los colores, en una algarabía insular pocas veces registrada en nuestra memoria colectiva. Mujer y juglar, juglar y griot, Excilia Saldaña diseñó un mapa bien claro por donde han ido desplazándose, sin cesar, los vientos aledaños al vórtice de un gran ciclón, el ciclón de su resistencia y de su metáfora andariega. Las alas de la maternidad la alcanzaron y por eso mismo emprendió vuelo hacia sí misma, hacia Ana Excilia, su abuela, hacia el vórtice de una violencia hija de ese primer capítulo de la tortura física que ensayaron la trata y la esclavitud. Incuestionablemente, esa experiencia histórica, estoy segura, moldeó el tema del cuerpo humano en la poesía de Excilia Saldaña. De ese holocausto histórico nació su conciencia del cuerpo; esa conciencia suministra a su escritura una gracia que la reafirma como una de las fundadoras del imaginario femenino cubano. De esos cuerpos lastrados por el látigo inmemorial, se nutren otros cuerpos—en primer lugar el suyo—hasta fundirse en uno solo, el cuerpo delirante del efebo en quien se inspira el poema "Mi fiel," escrito para celebrar sus cincuenta años en La Habana de 1996.

Este tratado erótico rompe todos los prognósticos, todas las leyes de la retórica y la academia, todas las concepciones del discurso poético femenino en Iberoamérica. No hay duda posible. Eros asoma su hocico en la punta del vórtice. Eros deambula por el mapa de Excilia y por nuestro archipiélago. En él ha podido encontrar, como premonición tal vez de su

troubadour's voice and that black accent that Nicolas Guillén had inaugurated into our poetry starting on April 20, 1930. Since the beginning, the vortex of her cyclone made her wander between the cultivation of her beautiful lullabies—with a formal grace truly enviable—and that free verse that, like a tropical epic, makes it possible for her to trace the map of an entire archipelago of civic, moral, and historical values. It is as if a blue bird, a bird of elegiac feathers, has flown over the map of the Island, saving itself from such human rending, from such familiar anguish, from such filial sentiments, in search of a more just and liberated country.

Excilia Saldaña was able to find the historical voice of the Cuban woman looking for her origin in slave ships, in those bitter crossings dating back to the sixteenth century, and who climbed the mountains during the two necessary wars in the nineteenth century. Out in the world she looked for an inheritance of oppression and she placed it before a mirror to show us how indebted we all are to that past of plundering and depredation, born in the plantations not only of Cuba but of the entire Caribbean and the black Americas.

Hers was a danzon macabre, danced by grandmothers and wives of all colors, in an insular clamor seldom registered in our collective memory. Woman and troubadour, troubadour and griot, Excilia Saldaña designed a very clear map where she has gradually shifted, without stopping, the winds adjoining the vortex of a great cyclone, the cyclone of her resistance and of her roving metaphor. The wings of maternity caught up with her and that is precisely why she took flight toward herself, toward Ana Excilia, her grandmother, toward the vortex of violence; daughter engendered of that first chapter of physical torture that slave trade and slavery practiced. Unquestionably, that historical experience, I am certain, shaped the theme of the human body in the poetry of Excilia Saldaña. From that historical holocaust was born her conscience of the body; and that conscience provides her writing with a grace that reaffirms her as one of the founders of the feminine Cuban imagination. Of those bodies ballasted by the immemorial lash, other bodies are nourished—to begin with hers—until they meld into one only, that of the desiring body of the ephebe who was the inspiration of her poem "My Faithful," written to celebrate her fiftieth birthday in Havana in 1996.

This erotic treatise ignores all weather forecasts, all laws of rhetoric and of the academy, all conceptions of feminine poetic discourse in Ibero-America. There is no doubt whatsoever. Eros directs its snout at the point

muerte, esa identidad que nació entre altas y bajas mareas, en bodegas de barcos sin destino, golpeada por latigazos que están por describir todavía. Ni siquiera los dioses han podido borrarlos de nuestra geografía, de nuestra historia existencial, de un yo atrofiado, acosado por *eros y tanatos*, como bien saben los griegos.

He amado esta voz poética y he aprendido de ella que mucha naturaleza nuestra, física y moral, se comporta de esa manera. Los poetas como ella la vencen, perfilándola, con su instrumento privilegiado que es la palabra en medio de estos mares y ríos por donde aún navega nuestra verdadera identidad. Ojalá la lectora y el lector de estos poemas puedan recibir la transparencia de estas ráfagas que nacen del corazón de Excilia Saldaña, muerta de risa cómplice, en el vórtice de su hermoso ciclón.

Nancy Morejón

Notas

1. Este poema, dedicado al poeta peruano César Calvo, fallecido en Lima en el año 2000, apareció publicado en la revista *Pájaro Cascabel*, D.F., n. 5-5, ene.–jul. de 1967, p. 43–46.

2. En Cuba, este es el nombre de una importante ceremonia *abakuá*.

of the vortex. Eros ambulates in Excilia's map, and in our archipelago. In it she has been able to find, perhaps as a premonition of her death, that identity that was born between high and low tides, in the cellar of ships without destiny, beaten by lashes yet to be described. Not even the gods have been able to erase them from our geography, from our existential history of an atrophied self, chased by *eros and thanatos*, as the Greeks well know.

I have loved this poetic voice and have learned from it that much of our moral and physical nature behaves in such a manner as hers. Poets like her vanquish it, profiling it with that privileged instrument that is the word in the middle of these seas and rivers where our true identity still navigates. Let us hope that the readers of these poems may receive the transparency of these wind gusts, born out of the heart of Excilia Saldaña, dying of her complicit laughter, in the vortex of her marvelous cyclone.

Nancy Morejón
Translation by Flora González Mandri and Rosamond Rosenmeier

Notes

1. This poem, dedicated to the Peruvian poet César Calvo, who died in Lima in 2000, was published in the journal *Pájaro Cascabel*, Mexico City, no. 5-5, January–July 1967, pp. 43–46.

2. In Cuba, this is the name of an important *abakuá* ceremony.

Translator's Note and Acknowledgments

I wish to acknowledge several grants from the Graduate Studies Office and Academic Affairs Office at Emerson College in Boston that allowed me to travel to Cuba in the eighties and nineties to meet and hold numerous conversations with Excilia Saldaña. Emerson College also contributed funds toward the preparation of the manuscript. The W.E.B. Du Bois Institute for Afro-American Research at Harvard University (1997–98), where I spent a year doing research, allowed me to bring Saldaña to the Boston area. I particularly wish to thank Richard Newman for his support.

Excilia Saldaña was extremely generous with her time and facilitated the acquisition of her books, a task that has grown increasingly difficult since 1989, when Cuba lost the Soviet economic subsidy and the U.S. economic embargo began to take its hold on the island nation. Mario Ernesto Romero provided me with information about his mother after her passing. *Gracias, Mario Ernesto.* I am indebted to Cintio Vitier for allowing me to reproduce the words he wrote in memory of Excilia Saldaña, published in *La Isla Infinita: Revista de Poesía* 1.2 (Julio–Diciembre, 1999): 33. I also wish to thank the following people who made it possible for Cintio Vitier's contribution and permission to travel between Havana and Cambridge: José Adrián Vitier (editor of *La Isla Infinita*), Lizzete Vila, Debra Evenson, Consuelo Ramírez Enríquez, and her son Alejandro.

I became an avid reader of Excilia Saldaña in the mid-eighties and have since then bemoaned the lack of translations of her works into English. During that time, only the poems of her contemporary Nancy Morejón were readily available under the title *Where the Island Sleeps Like a Wing* (Black Scholar Press, 1985). A few of Saldaña's works now appear

in English in anthologies by Pedro Pérez Sarduy and Jean Stubbs, by Ruth Behar and Juan León, by Amanda Hopkinton and by Margaret Randall. I felt compelled to make known here in the United States some of what I consider to be her best work, during a period when African American women writers have established themselves with works that deal with the same issues of race, cultural heritage, and gender. The figure of Alice Walker and her relationship with her mother as a source of strength and creative inspiration comes prominently to mind, but there are too many to mention here.

Because of my academic training, I felt limited in my capacity to translate a poet whose strong voice relies so heavily on complex rhythms and rhymes inherent in children's and traditional poetry. I was thus overjoyed when Rosamond Rosenmeier, personal friend and accomplished poet, expressed interest in a collaborative venture. I would always start with a near literal translation of the work, and send it to Rosamond with a taped reading of the poem in Spanish; these steps would begin a mutual process of formulating the translations that are presented here. As we put our collective minds and languages together, brand new readings of the poems emerged. Rosamond and I are very grateful for the invaluable comments by Excilia Saldaña on her reading of the translations. We are also indebted to Susan Fernández of the University Press of Florida and to all of the anonymous readers who helped us acknowledge our limitations. Priscilla Long provided much needed advice in our "last" revision of the manuscript. My flawed photographic image of Excilia Saldaña was much improved through the digital know-how of Hui Yeng Chang. Thanks also to Don Gurewitz for lending his photographic expertise under pressure of time. *Gracias,* Alexis Esquivel, for your powerful image, *Iyá.*

Rosamond and I also thank Saul Slapikoff for his editorial and technical expertise as well as for his wonderful meals while Rosamond, Excilia, and I worked. His commitment to Saldaña's work is equal to Rosamond's and mine. He and Excilia shared many early breakfasts together; their competency in their respective foreign languages, English and Spanish, improved during the poet's stay at our home. Saul's help, persistence, and encouragement during the time of manuscript preparation attests to his friendship with Excilia.

The process of translation for me also included countless trips to libraries and to Afro-Cuban communities from one end of the island to the other to get a clearer sense of the multiple African heritages that coexist

in my native country. Translating Saldaña's poetry has meant an apprenticeship for me, a coming to terms with an Afro-Cuban tradition that I had acknowledged before only through the richness of our music. In respect for that tradition, our translations have left Afro-Cuban terms intact. A glossary of those voices is included at the end of the book. I thank Rosamond for lending me her poetic ear and imagination so strongly rooted as well in the domestic and the mythic. As we all know, translations always betray the original. I only hope that this collaborative effort of a Cuban-American reader and a North American poet conveys the best of Saldaña's voice.

Introduction

Excilia Saldaña (b. 1946), was an accomplished Cuban poet, translator, essayist, university professor (Universidad Pedagógica de Santa Clara), and member of the editorial board Editorial Gente Nueva in Havana. She died in Havana on July 20, 1999, from complications suffered as a result of a severe asthma attack. The next day, Mercedes Santos Moray declared in *Juventud Rebelde*, "Your friends, your comrades, your son, your readers, have not lost you because you have overcome death with life, a life that pulses and will endure in your works."[1] In homage to Saldaña, writer and critic Consuelo Ramírez Enríquez wrote in the short story "El vientre del pez" (The Belly of the Fish):

> she cultivated plants and friendships, collected glass and wrought iron fences, gave classes on grammar and tenderness, assembled books by the hundreds, and from her noble and panting breath, from her clean and breathless chest, from her bosom always in silent torture, she tore out verses and more verses, and more verses. ...Verses that if written in small letters could well reach around the entire island—if only people understood that this is not a metaphor! That when it seemed that she had emptied her chest, her heaving chest, without air, drowned in asthma and in torture, new, even more beautiful verses emerged, surprisingly beautiful, because her bosom was a well with its bed in the INFINITE.[2]

During her lifetime, Excilia Saldaña struggled to make her works known in the Americas as much as she struggled with her breath—in spite of the fact that her children's books have been translated in several Eastern and Western European countries, in spite of the fact that "The Wife's Monologue," *Kele Kele*, and *La Noche* have been staged in Cuba and Sweden, in spite of the fact that she has received multiple prizes in

her homeland, including the Premio Rosa Blanca, Premio Nacional Ismaelillo, Premio La Edad de Oro for her children's books, as well as the Nicolás Guillén Distinction for Poetry in 1998, given by the UNEAC (National Union of Cuban Writers and Artists).

In the Vortex of the Cyclone, containing translations of some of her major works, including two autobiographical poems, samples of her children's poetry, an erotic letter, and a few poems representative of her voice from the beginning and the end of her poetic career, hopes to ensure that her words will endure for English and Spanish speakers alike.

Since the 1980s, several critics have given attention to interpretations of her poetry. The work of Catherine Davies, for example, places her in the context of women writers in twentieth-century Cuba and points to her Afrocentric definition of the Cuban female subject within a national and international context.[3]

My own critical interest in Saldaña's poetry centers around her repeated attempts at defining the autobiographical and poetic self. In her search for her own signature, Saldaña echoes and transforms masters from a wide range of literary traditions, including Shakespeare, Quevedo, Sor Juana Inés de la Cruz, Walt Whitman, Nicolás Guillén, Lydia Cabsrera, Vicente Huidobro, Martí, Lezama Lima, García Lorca, Dora Alonso, Renée Potts, Mirta Aguirre, and many others. When speaking about her poetic indebtedness, Saldaña stated, in her essay "The Transcendent Quotidian: Reflections on my Poetic Works":[4]

> As a writer, I feel indebted to everyone. The list is going to be endless. As far as my family is concerned, to Ana Excilia—grandmother, and to my grandfather Esteban. To my mother; to the incentive of a relative whom I never knew, but who is one of the protagonists of Cuban culture: Juan Francisco Sariol, editor of *Orto*, the journal from Manzanillo. As far as my DNA goes, to my maternal grandmother, about whom they say that she filled notebooks with poems and delivered lectures at the Rotary Club, in spite of being black as night, or rather, of being "the little Congo woman," as she was called. I did not know her, but she navigates in my blood. As far as the universal literary family, I'm indebted to everyone who wrote and whom I have read. As far as the Cuban literary family: Nicolás, Lezama, all of Orígenes, Ballagas, Brull, Mirta, Dora, the two Renées, Onelio . . . Of the contemporary ones I say nothing, but without plagiarizing them, I assert that I have incorporated them

all. I have learned something from all of them, and I admire them for the humility with which they give themselves, for the goodness and the love that they have toward children.

Just recently I found out that I owed much to film and dance: the turns of Alicia Alonso, of ballet in general, are the turns with which I dream. They are the turns of the flight of poetry.

And to Martí, of course. (p. 11)

In response to the statement by the Cuban critic Virgilio López Remus that "Excilia Saldaña is a living classic of literature written for children and young adults," Saldaña responded:

I am not a classic. Martí is a classic, one who has been proven to be by time, nation and ideology. To say of me that I am a classic is a metaphor, not an axiom, and I hope it will not become a sophism. I am a lady who wishes to write poetry. I have the wish, although I lack the instrument like the cinematographic Saliery. I am someone with a lot of fear of being mistaken, and someone with a lot of persistence. I am not [a classic]. I hope my books will be. (p. 11)

Excilia Saldaña weaves the personal, the mythical, and the literary in an attempt to bring together the domestic and the transcendental, the temporal and the eternal. She defines poetry as a perpetual search for the transcendent quotidian:

I prefer to baptize this search as a form of internalism, because what I look for is roots, what I look for is the internal essence of poetry. In other words: poetry without boundaries, be it in prose or in verse, and even in its self-reflection; in a way this poetic reflection could be indebted to the poetic image of Lezama Lima, only that this internalization, this internalist poetry is rooted in the senses, in reality. It is not in the image but in its becoming that it finds its full incarnation. Sometime in some conference about my work, I classified it as the transcendent quotidian, or what is the same, as the task of ordinary people which is an expression of a greater spiritual task, the order of life to find the cosmic order. Because of that, I am sustained, or rather, my poetry is sustained by an ethics, by a morality that is the essence itself of our national identity. (p. 8)

This link between her quotidian poetic reality and Cuban national identity finds expression in the poet's inventive search for an image that

fuses the self with the island and the literary heritage founded by Martí: "I am the Night. I am the Island. / Two homelands contained in me." (Unfinished Danzon for Night and Island).

*   *   *

In this brief autobiographical statement from Excilia Saldaña's collection of children's poems, *La Noche,* the personal becomes the mythical:

> I was born August 7, 1946, at six in the afternoon when the sun was about ready to give way to Night. Then she arrived: from the adolescent arms of my mother I went to hers, arms made to be grandmother's: my grandmother. Now, when I see her in photographs, I see an ageless woman, ruddy and healthy like any daughter of a Caribbean mulatto woman and of an islander. She is no longer; some gold bracelets, a broken pitcher and the profile of my son remain. But, isn't memory the presence of the heart? She lives on. I have my strange name which is hers, and the memories: unwithering, ours.
>
> In the old house of La Víbora, or under the huge porch in Santa Fé, I learned her word and her silence. And the best part of me.[5]

The gesture of the infant's being handed over into the grandmother's arms signifies not only the giving of the baby to the grandmother's care, but also the gesture of the child's being handed into the Afro-Cuban tradition. This transition from the personal to the mythical sphere is made concrete with the image of the photograph bearing "an ageless woman," born out of the figure that reinvents the origin of Cuban culture, the mulatto woman, product of the imposed miscegenation of the Spanish and the African.

The gold bracelets and the broken pitcher, fragments of the past, represent the grandmother's presence, as does her profile projected in Saldaña's son. In this prose poem, Excilia Saldaña positions herself as the link to a past that—but for the memories engraved in the poet's imagination—could be erased. The future depends on the poet's ability to nurture it with her own words.

The grandmother's image in the poet's name, "my strange name," and in the sounds and silences of the grandmother's voice, has given Saldaña "the best part of me," her poetic idiom. At sites of the domestic and the public, the poet-grandchild receives the oral tradition, in the house and

on the porch. In Saldaña's poetry, female traditions are literally handed down with a loving gesture, from the interior to the exterior, and are given oral and written voice.

Recreating the grandmother's voice and silences in the written poetic word, Excilia Saldaña has published a series of children's books, including *La Noche*, which consists of poetic conversations between an inquiring child-self and the grandmother whose wise aphorisms instruct the granddaughter: "—What is poetry, Grandma? I want to know. / —It is not rhyme. No. / —If not, what is it? Tell me, since you know and I need to / know. / —It's verse. / —What it is, and what it is not. Such a mystery! / —That's precisely what poetry is!" (p. 34).

The poems collected in *In the Vortex of the Cyclone* present Saldaña as a multifaceted poet. She is a poet's poet in that she constantly dialogues with a wide-ranging literary tradition, both Western and non-Western, yet also endeavors to speak through a language that is at times colloquial, at times domestic. Like Nicolás Guillén, she is at home in the Cuban vernacular. Her lullabies attest to her commitment to children much as did the lullabies of her Cuban predecessors José Martí and Georgina Herrera, and of the Chilean Gabriela Mistral. "Through the Looking Glass" plays with poetic language as paradox in the mode of Lewis Carroll. The erotic letter, excerpt of an erotic memoir, appeals to the vocal forcefulness of Pablo Neruda and Walt Whitman, and represents an ironic rendering of the canvases of Georgia O'Keefe. In all these instances, Saldaña transforms existing artistic traditions by placing herself as a woman of the African diaspora at the center of her poetic self-identification. The strongest poems in this collection, "The Wife's Monologue" and *My Name (A Family Anti-Elegy)*, project the image of a woman poet's memory—what she calls "the tresses of my memory"—and of the grandmother as Afro-Cuban mythical figure.

"The Wife's Monologue," first published in the Cuban journal *Casa de las Américas* in 1985, unlocks the gates of Saldaña's past by appealing first to the men in her history.[6] The question—"Who gilded my hands with blood?"—remains central but unanswered by any of the male figures who inhabited both her domestic spaces and the wider world. Finally, lost "in some corner complaining," the poet finds the key, a rusty key used by her mother and her grandmother, and her grandmother's grandmothers, both the Castilian and the Carabalí, the European and the African. The answer that will heal the wounded self comes not from her

male ancestry, but from the common experience shared by the Afro-Caribbean woman: the sexual violation by "a flamenco gypsy dancer" in an afternoon of children's games and nursery rhymes. Saldaña binds her experience of incest to a common past in that Caribbean culture, and her poem thus acquires mythical dimensions. Even though, at the end, the woman with the stained hands appeals to a Husband to join her in the cleansing of her past, it is the work of the artist evoked in the feminine gesture of the opening metaphor that has the true power to heal: "I am a watery child, as well, / braiding and unbraiding / the tresses of my memory."

Excilia Saldaña, like her Cuban mentor and predecessor Nicolás Guillén, celebrates her African ancestry by populating her poem with the flora and fauna symbolically drawn from Afro-Cuban rituals and by quoting and transforming Hispanic masters. Even the Cuban reader must consult *El Monte* (The Sacred Wild) by Lydia Cabrera, a monumental ethnographic text that recalls the voices of many Afro-Cuban informants regarding the African rites and rituals in the diaspora.[7] Like Guillén, who often wrote verses in traditional Hispanic forms, Saldaña alludes to an all-encompassing poetic tradition, from Shakespeare to García Lorca.[8] Thus, "The Wife's Monologue," for example, echoes Federico García Lorca's "Lament for Ignacio Sánchez Mejías." Saldaña's initial refusal to see the shamed girl as she appears in her memory "(But no, I do not want to see her!)," is a revision of Lorca's famous line. Saldaña is indebted to Guillén for his integration of African and Hispanic cultural traditions in poetry, as *mestizaje*, but she brings to the forefront the force of the feminine heritage in the Caribbean basin.

Saldaña's lengthy elegy, *My Name (A Family Anti-Elegy)*, published in 1991 by Ediciones Unión, bears a dedication to both Guillén and her grandmother Ana Excilia Bregante.[9] While establishing a direct correlation with Nicolás Guillén's "The Last Name: A Family Elegy" (1951), this poem, like "The Wife's Monologue," constitutes a rejection of the male tradition and foregrounds a female tradition in an act of poetic self-definition. Even though it is with Guillén that Saldaña explicitly dialogues here, she repeatedly refers to the Creationist posture of the Chilean poet Vicente Huidobro, a contemporary of Guillén who conceived of the poetic voice as creator of the universe through the act of naming. When Saldaña rejects Guillén and adapts Huidobro's stance, she does so to establish her name as the ultimate source of life for her poetry. Like Walt

Whitman in "Song of Myself," Saldaña sets out to recreate the world of the Caribbean basin by the persistent invocation of her name. Saldaña's elegy thus ends: "My name / to precipitate like rain on the *cántaro* of my archipelago." Saldaña's grand poetic strategy is to accomplish no less than the displacing of Huidobro and Guillén, two major poets in Latin America's Vanguard tradition. To do so Saldaña repeatedly appeals to the mythical figure of her grandmother. Under the guise of rescuing her grandmother's forgotten and unusual name, Saldaña names herself: "I save you / and I save my name from oblivion and hell."

My Name begins by recording the dichotomy in the poetic self between hostile reality and creative imagination. The self will eventually find wholeness through grounding the name in personal experience, historic reality, and, finally, Caribbean geography. The narrative of the poem begins by establishing a closed environment within the family household where the female child grows in a hostile atmosphere: "My house is Hell's first stop." The father is absent yet he is present through unspoken fears. This poem, unlike "The Wife's Monologue," which clearly refers to incest, veils the act of incest through the image of father and daughter dancing a round: "They never / stopped the circle. No they never / dressed me in white / or / scrubbed my skin to transparency."

Poetic consciousness is born by tracing a female family history beginning with the grandmother's conception, an event that coincides with the nation's birth at the beginning of the century: "A mistake / the sultriest afternoon in August / of this century born under the fanfare / and the Amendment." Here Saldaña refers to the Platt Amendment, which was attached to Cuba's initial constitution, allowing the United States to intervene in Cuba's national affairs for U.S. security reasons. In this context, the grandmother was born at a time of national betrayal: "It was my time to lose."

In the progressive spiral of history, the granddaughter, who is ten when Fidel Castro's revolutionary movement begins in 1956, hopes her life and the life of the nation will be marked by a period of redemption. *My Name* records young Saldaña's rebellion as she favors a political struggle that her middle-class family rejects. Within the private spaces of the family house, the poet-child experiences her body, her bouts with asthma, her coming into womanhood, and her sexuality. Only the young child seems to notice that while the family celebrates a Christmas Eve feast inside, "the Island walks on tears."

Ultimately, as the enemy within the household, she must lead a double life, inside as besieged daughter, and outside, as revolutionary: "Suddenly / girls decide not to die of love or of anemia: / On the streets they march like flags." She finds comfort in her grandmother, who although refusing to join Saldaña in her fervor, serves as an unconditional supporter of her poetic endeavor. Saldaña wields her pen as a poetic weapon, like a hopeful soldier as she quotes San Juan de la Cruz: "But, / stand aside. / I'm going with my pen. / But, / stand aside. / I'm in a hurry and I fly / with a loving rifle in my hand / beehiving the honey I carry inside." The poetic, the historical, the political, and the feminine coincide in this one defiant stanza. The act of poetic creation, of naming, is centered in the experience of procreation: "I am free within the space / of the first freedom / to encounter my origin / in the son who engenders me."

Having rejected her family, after being rejected by them, she is engendered by the future generation that she brings into life. The woman poet achieves freedom by tearing down cultural values that present a contradiction between living in domestic spaces and participating in historic events. In the acts of child bearing and literary creation, Saldaña wields her signature so that through the poetic conception of her name she can transcend her physical, historic, and geographic limitations while living within them. By consciously accepting her grandmother's name, Excilia, this Afro-Cuban poet assumes her condition of being exiled in her asthmatic body and in her home. By the end of the poem, Saldaña has created her own archipelago.

Flora González Mandri

Paisaje anónimo

Cada tarde
la mujer se sienta
           frente a la ventana abierta
culpable de no ser aire, agua, nube
      —o al menos ala que vuela—
de ser sólo una mujer frente a una ventana abierta.

Cada tarde
el cielo se orea
          tras la ventana abierta
avergonzado de no ser hombre, carne, cuerpo
      —o al menos tierra—
de ser solamente cielo tras una ventana abierta.

Pasión clandestina de culpa y vergüenza:
una mujer dorada y un cielo violeta,
cada tarde, a través de una ventana abierta.

- written when she was 18 - won a prize
for the collection, but decided not
to publish it

Anonymous Landscape

- like sonnet - 1st 2 stanzas
make statements,
3rd bring them
together

Every afternoon
the woman sits
　　　before the open window
guilty of not being air, water, cloud
　　　—or at least a wing that flies—
of being only a woman before an open window.

Every afternoon
the sky hangs itself out to dry
　　　beyond the open window
ashamed of not being man, flesh, body
　　　—or at least earth—
of being only sky beyond an open window.

Secret passion of guilt and shame:
a golden woman and a violet sky,
every afternoon, through an open window.

- self portrait
- patakines - longing for what you are not
- not appreciating what you are -
looking at the are - not seeing
how beautiful you are

soothing, yet there's guilt,
shame + secret
- not exposed, just there

- not alone in
feelings of
guilt and
shame, even
though they're
traditionally
very personal
- reflection of
one another -
- defined by
absence
frame of window limits

Monólogo de la esposa

—Pero, ¿crees tú que, cuando una se casa . . .
es así como ella dice?

Miguel de Carrión: *Las honradas*

Los crespos de la noche cuelgan del cielo.
Se esparcen por los hombros de la casa las guedejas
del silencio.
Yo las peino. Suavemente yo las peino:
Soy la anónima alisadora de las ondas del sueño.
también soy una niña acuática
trenzando y destrenzándome
la cabellera del recuerdo.

A veces me paro en los acantilados del hogar
y los aciclono hasta convertirlos en cumbres borrascosas:

        Vengan huracán y lamento
        a soplar sobre la mentira.
        Lo que no me niega la vida
        lo niego yo a cada momento.

O los oreo por verles florecer las piedras:

        Vengan la brisa y la porfía
        a soplar sobre la verdad.
        Lo que a mí me niega tu faz
        no lo niego yo a la alegría.

Entonces se acercan monjes
                de extraños ritos,
      se acercan juglares
               y músicos,
      se acercan mujeres gordas
                y jóvenes entecos
      a preguntar la fórmula mágica
             de mis vientos.

The Wife's Monologue

"But, do you believe that when you marry . . .
it's like the way she says it is?"

Miguel de Carrión: *The Honest Women.*

The curls of night hang from the sky.
The long tresses of silence are loosened on the shoulders of the
    house.
I comb them. Softly I comb them:
I am the anonymous one who smooths the waves of sleep.
I am a watery child, as well,
braiding and unbraiding
the tresses of my memory.

At times I stand on my home cliffs
and storm at them until I turn them into my own wuthering
    heights.

        Let hurricanes and lamentations
        blow upon all lies.
        What life does not deny me
        I myself deny at every moment.

At times I set them out to dry to see them bloom from stones.

        Let soft winds and persistence
        blow upon the truth.
        What your countenance denies me
        I will not deny to joy.

Then, come monks of
            strange rituals,
    then come troubadours
            and musicians,
    then come fat women
            and also sickly young men
    asking for the magic formula
            of my breezes.

"Hermanos, no hay receta, es que soy en la vida:
canto mi minuto en la gran fiesta cósmica.
El vuelo del pájaro en busca del aire
es la expresión de mi libertad;
la sumisión de la bestia
es el dibujo de mi poderío;
la vileza de la serpiente
reafirma mi nobleza.
Yo estoy en la vida saboreando cada uno de sus tiempos
como estaré en la muerte solazándome de la eternidad.
Me niego a estar en los umbrales."

Sé que los confundo
porque cierto ramo de mariposas
endulza una fosa abierta.
¿Qué cloqueo de huesos lejanos fue
carne y crimen sobre mis ijares?

Las manos. Las manos. Las manos.

No hay agua suficiente para limpiar mis manos,
para desteñir el estigma de sangre
               —de mi propia sangre—
tañendo para siempre mis manos.

Soy yo. La Esposa:

               Silencio:
               Oigo un ruido:
Mis pobrecitos candidatos a muertos
               tocan a la puerta.
Visto rápidamente mis hábitos de sacerdotisa.
               Debo abrir:
"Pasen ahora y dejen sus ofrendas votivas,
cumplan sus promesas:
Papayas y ciruelas y caimitos
y conchas y panecillos calientes y jícaras:
mis símbolos en oro y metales bastardos.
Toquen la punta de mi delantal,

"Brothers, there is no recipe. It's only that I am in life.
I sing my moment in the great cosmic feast.
The flight of the bird in search of air
is the expression of my freedom;
the obedience of the beast
is the pattern of my power;
the vileness of the serpent
reaffirms my nobility.
I am in life savoring each of its stages
as in death I will enjoy its eternity.
I refuse to stand in thresholds."

I know that I confuse them
because a certain bouquet of butterflies[1]
sweetens an open grave.
What clacking of far away bones was
meat and crime upon my loins?

My hands. My hands. My hands.

There is not water enough to cleanse my hands,
to bleach the stain
            —the stigma of my own blood—
drumming forever on my hands.

It is I. The Wife.

                    Silence!
            I hear a noise:
My poor little candidates for death
                    knocking at the door.
I quickly don my priestess robes.
                    I must open the door.
"Come in. Leave your votive gifts,
fulfill your promises:
Papayas and figs and star apples
and shells and warm loaves and small gourds,
my symbols in gold and base metals.
Touch the edges of my apron,

besen mis chancletas rotas de plástico,
corten mis callos como reliquia,
enciendan las escobas y los trapeadores,
capa y cetro de plumero y bayeta,
corónenme con dedales,
acaricien las agujas de mi costado.
Esperen el milagro."

Desde el templo que me erijo, permanezco
en el ara de mi costumbre, vestal
inextinguible de la llama
del fogón:
        leño,
            alcohol,
                  keroseno,
                      o gas

no faltará a terapeutas y frustrados,
        locos y cobardes,
        pregoneros y borrachos,
        impotentes y poetas.

Soy la diosa tutelar de la Avenida de los Dolores:
mater familias de un abolengo de matarifes;
en la diestra el cuchillo
                     y en la siniestra la res.

Las manos. Las manos. Las manos.
¿Qué gloria pisoteará el laurel?
¿Qué llanto culpable plañirá la cebolla?
¿Qué dentadura feroz me mostrará el ajo
más temible que estas manos manchadas de sangre?

Soy yo. La Esposa.
Estoy segura de serlo. No
me gusta engañarme aunque a veces crea
que tocan a la puerta, y sólo el viento
o
mi deseo de compañía
froten sus nudillos contra la madera.

cinderella?

kiss my broken plastic slippers,
trim my corns out as if they were relics,
set my mops and brooms on fire,
my dust-mop, cape and feather scepter,
crown me with thimbles,
caress the needles piercing my sides.
Wait for the miracle."

From the temple that I build, I remain permanently
in the altar of my familiar,
inextinguishable vestal from the flame
in my stove:

$$\text{No firewood,}$$
$$\text{alcohol,}$$
$$\text{kerosene,}$$
$$\text{or gas}$$

shall be withheld from counsellors, from the frustrated,
crazy and cowardly,
from peddlers and drunkards,
from the impotent and the poets.

I am the tutelar goddess of the Avenida de los Dolores:
mater familias of a lineage of butchers:
in my right hand the knife
in my left the beef.

lady macb

My hands. My hands. My hands.
What glories will the laurel trample under foot?
What guilty tears will the onion weep?
What ferocious fangs will the garlic bear
more feared than these blood-stained hands?

It is I. The Wife.
I am certain of it. No, I don't
like to deceive myself but at times I think
someone's knocking at my door, and is it only the wind
or
my desire for company
which scours its knuckles against the wood?

La soledad es peor que la muerte.
La muerte es sólo una trampa en el bosque
para cazar al cervatillo:
                el fin de la huida.
Pero la soledad es la persecución y el dolor:
conozco su himplar
                entre las ramas de la loza,
veo sus ojos amarillos
                sopesarme entre sartenes y sombras,
acaricio su lomo sedoso
                en un claro de la sopa.
Y allí recojo y guardo sus lágrimas dentro de un cántaro enano,
un cántaro enano que alimenta una fuente,
una fuente que surte un río,
un río que llena un mar,
un mar que cabe en un ojo,
un ojo que llora dentro de un cántaro enano
todo el dolor.

Las manos. Las manos. Las manos.
¿No he de ver limpias estas manos?

Soy yo. La Esposa.
Todo el dolor del mundo vino a pedir mi mano:
"No soy la Novia," le dije, "sino la Esposa,
¿puedes tú lavarme las manos?
¿Hay dolor suficiente para limpiar mis manos?"

Pero el dolor sólo cava y zanja sobre el pecho
su jornada abismal,
su oficio de agujero.
Sembrador de tempestades, agricultor
de duelos. Su viña que nadie quiere,
él la cuida con esmero.

El dolor nunca está ocioso:
Los holgazanes son los muertos.
Pero no en las tumbas.

Loneliness is worse than death.
Death is only a snare in the woods
set to catch a new-born fawn:
                                    the end of the chase.
But loneliness is persecution and pain:
I know its roar
                        amidst the styles of the porcelain,
I see its yellow eyes
                    appraising me between frying pans and shadows,
I caress its silky back
                            in the clearing of the soup.
And there I gather and keep its tears in a toy pitcher,
a toy pitcher that nourishes a fountain,
a fountain that feeds a river,
a river that fills a sea,
a sea that fits in an eye,
an eye that cries inside a toy pitcher
all of the pain.

My hands. My hands. My hands.
Will I ever see these hands clean?

It is I. The Wife.
All the pain in the world came to ask for my hand:
"I am not the Bride," I told them, "but the Wife.
Can you cleanse my hands?
Is there pain enough to cleanse my hands?"

But pain only digs and carves on my chest
its abysmal day's work,
its labor as hole-maker,
as sower of storms, as harvester
of duels. His vineyard—that nobody wants—
he cares for it meticulously.

Pain is never idle:
The lazy ones are the dead ones.
But not in tombs.

O en los mausoleos.
O en las ánforas
donde la ceniza se acomoda
al culto ancestral, al renacimiento totémico.
En los cementerios no descansan los muertos:
Cada nicho es el cuartel de un general;
cada epitafio, la clarinada para un ejército.
(Desde allí galopan en corceles esqueléticos
para invadir las ciudades, las leyendas y los recuerdos.)
No, los muertos no descansan en los cementerios.
Su lugar de reposo son las tendederas,
en la democracia del alambre y la soga
—donde conviven el paño lujoso y el jirón maltrecho.
En la némesis del sol descansan los muertos.
De la bondad, del olvido, de la furia, de la paz
descansan los muertos.
¡Qué acto de amor incomparable es plancharlos luego!
Almidonados y lisos
—colgados
por orden de colores
en los percheros—
listos están siempre en mi armario, para usarlos
si los vivos se queman en mi infierno:
muertos de verano
y de invierno,
muertos de estreno
y de uso,
smuertos de andar
y de domingo:
mis muertos, mis pobrecitos muertos saludables,
mis fantasmas del colchón y el sueño.

Las manos. Las manos. Las manos.
¿Con qué detergente arrancar la costra de sangre de mis manos?

"Soy yo. La Esposa,"
escribí un día en cientos de tarjetas,
"los convoco a la hora nonata a una asamblea."

                    Or in mausoleums.
Or in amphoras
                    where the ashes find comfort
in their ancestral cult, their totemic renaissance.
In cemeteries the dead do not rest:
Each niche is the barracks of a general;
each epitaph, the clarion for an army.
(From there, they gallop on skeletal steeds
to invade cities, legends and memories.)
No, the dead do not rest in cemeteries.
Their resting places are clotheslines,
in the democracy of wires and ropes
—where luxurious cloth and frayed tatters live together.
The dead rest in the nemesis of the sun.
From kindness, from forgetfulness, from fury, from peace,
the dead rest.
What an incomparable act of love it is to iron them, then!
Starched and smooth
—hung out
                    in order of color
on their hangers—
they hang in my closet ready to wear
if the live ones burn in my hell:
                    dead from summer
                              and from winter
                    dead from brand new
                              and used clothes
                    dead from everyday clothes
                              and from Sunday best:
my dead, my little poor healthy dead,
my ghosts of the mattress and sleep.

My hands. My hands. My hands.
What detergent would remove the blood crust from my hands?

"It is I. The Wife,"
I wrote in hundreds of notecards,
"I summon you to an assembly at an unborn hour."

Vestí
        de malva y heliotropo,
me toqué
                con orquídeas y violetas,
calcé
        berenjenas moradas,
alfombré
                la casa hasta la bañadera.

Cada cual llegó con su voz y sus manías,
cada cual llegó con sus manías y sus maneras:
el adolescente lánguido y felino,
                el insolente y atlético;
el joven hirsuto y barbado,
                el lampiño y sereno;
el poeta de juegos florales,
                el poeta de los florilegios;
el caballero cansado,
                el gallardo caballero:
mi casa llena de espectros.

Los vehementes me tomaban del talle
y prendían en mi escote hipsipilas violentas:

                ¡Que dance, que cante!
                ¡Que alegre la fiesta!

Los tímidos sonreían y echaban a volar
sobre el griterío, tataguas silenciosas y ciegas:

                ¡Que no dance, que no cante!
                ¡Que sea sólo, que sea!

Menos alucinada que Ofelia,
más transformada que Aldonza,
tan aguerrida como Julieta
—bíblica, clásica, retrechera—
con los pies ligeros,
sin ningún buey sobre mi lengua
exclamé:

I dressed in
            mauve and heliotrope
I dabbed myself
            with orchids and violets,
I covered my feet
            with purple eggplants,
I carpeted
            the house up to the bathtub.

Each one arrived with his voice and his whims
each one arrived with his whims and his ways:
the languid and feline adolescent,
            the insolent and the athlete;
the hairy and bearded young man,
            the hairless and the serene;
the poet of poetry contests
            and the poet of Golden Treasuries;
the tired gentleman,
            the elegant gentleman:
my house full of specters.

The fervent ones held me by the waist
and on my neckline pinned furious hipsipilas:

            Let her dance, let her sing!
            Let her brighten the fiesta!

The shy ones smiled and began to flee
above the uproar, like giant hipsipilas, silent and blind:

            Do not dance, do not sing!
            Let her only be, let her be!

Less hallucinated than Ophelia,
more transformed than Aldonza,
as embattled as Juliet
—biblical, classical, cunning—
with light feet,
with no ox on my tongue
I exclaimed:

Ay,
>mis muertos,
como decíamos ayer: veinte años no es nada.
¿Dónde los perdí la vez postrera?
¿Quién fue que así mató nuestro destino sin razón?
¿Acaso un dios envidioso,
>un dios desprovisto de piedad
>un dios eunuco de corazón y sexo?
¿O fuimos nosotros
>>—Sanchos y Quijotes de la mácula—
quienes convertimos un noble gigante
en tosco molino de viento?
>Ay,
>>mis muertos,
mis deseosos en el retrato ovalado de mi pecho:
Toda mujer ama lo que mata,
>Ay,
>>mis muertos,
la pobre mulatica bizca,
>>>centro de burla del colegio,
que quiso ser princesa de un exótico reino
que custodian cien blancos con sus cien alabardas,
un sijú que no duerme y un otá colosal,
es ahora la reina viuda de tantos empeños.
>Ay,
>>mis muertos,
que se acerque el que tomó mi doncellez,
la oscura magnolia de mi vientre,
que venga a desposarme el primero
>>>para que le pueda ver
los ojos,
>>>para que le pueda ver
las manos,
>>>para que le pueda ver,
aunque un sol de alacranes me coma la sien.
>Ay,
>>mis muertos,
¿quién es el primero?

Ah,
             my dead ones,
as we used to say: twenty years is nothing.[2]   *verse from famous tango*
Where did I lose sight of them back then?
Who was it who killed our future without reason?
Could it have been an envious god,
             a pitiless god,
a god eunuch of sex and heart?
Or was it us
                —Sanchos and Quixotes of all blemish—
who turned a noble giant
into a rough windmill?
             Ah,
                my dead ones,
my wishful ones centered in the oval frame of my breast:
Every woman loves what she kills.
             Ah,
                my dead ones,
the poor cross-eyed little mulatta,   —▷ *herself*
                  the laughing-stock at school,
who wanted to be princess of an exotic kingdom
kept by a hundred white men with their hundred halberds,
by a wakeful gnome owl and a colossal otá—
she's now the widowed queen of so many pledges.
             Ah,
                my dead ones,
let the one who took my virginity come forth,
the dark magnolia of my womb,
let him who was first, marry me,
                  so I may see
his eyes,
                  so I may see
his hands,
                  so I may see him,
even though a scorpion sun eats at my temples.
             Ah,
                my dead ones,
who is the first?

¿Quién es el primero,
infancia de azabache y cieno?
¿Tú, adolescente, flor, cáncer?

            ¿O tú, cabeza de fuego,
llama de la infidelidad de tu madre?
¿Tú, con tu neurosis de pacotilla

            y tus alardes?
¿O tú, de quien tengo un hijo,

          aliento de mi aire,
un hijo que se te parece,

         pero quien te niega en mi talle?
¿Quién es el primero?

        ¿Quién talla en los corales
mis piernas, extrañas calles?
¿Quién es el primero?

        ¿Quién escribe con mis senos
elegía de nata y ayes?
¿Quién me convoca en sus noches?
¿Quién me traiciona en sus tardes?
¿Quién desprecia el azor

        por no cazarme?
¿Quién se apena de ser lobo

         tras aullarme?
¿Quién quisiera tener un falo de hiedra,

          para treparme?
¿Quién fue,

    quién es,

        quién será el primero?

¿Quién me doró las manos de sangre?

Soy yo. La Esposa.
Mas la respuesta no estaba entre los muertos.

Vértigo.

Entonces salí a la calle a preguntar
al médico y al bodeguero:
"Paciente, tiene un enfisema, pero lo peor
es que le falta el ovario derecho."

Who is the first,
infant of jet and slime?
Or you, adolescent, flower, cancer?
                    Or you, head of fire,
flame of your mother's infidelity?
You, with your second-rate neurosis
                    and your ostentation?

Or you, from whom I have a son,
                    spirit of my breath,
a son who resembles you,
                    but who, having my stature, denies you?
Who is the first?
                    Who carves on coral,
my legs, strange streets?
Who is the first?
                    Who writes with my breasts
an elegy of cream and sighs?
Who summons me in his nights?
Who betrays me in his afternoons?
Who scorns the goshawk
                    for not hunting me?
Who is ashamed of being a wolf
                    after howling at me?
Who would like to have an ivy phallus
                    to climb on me?
Who was,
        who is,
            who will be the first?

Who gilded my hands with blood?

It is I. The Wife.
But the answer was not to be found among the dead.

Vertigo.

Then I went out on the streets to ask
the doctor and the shopkeeper:
"Patient, you have emphysema, but the worst is
you are missing your right ovary."

"Marchante, puede pagarme la sal,
pero para la miel no le llega el dinero."

Entonces salí a la calle a preguntar
al albañil y al plomero:
"Doña, lo mejor es tirar otra placa,
aunque si pone una viga se aguantan los techos."
"Tía, esa sifa todavía resiste,
apúrese y compre un meruco nuevo."

Entonces salí a la calle a preguntar
al maestro y al carpintero:
"Alumna, uno más uno es dos,
Dos por cero es cero."
"Casera, el barniz es sólo para dar brillo,
dele guerra al comején antes de que muera el madero."

Entonces salí a la calle a preguntar
al campesino y al artillero:
"Comay, la siembra depende de uno,
la cosecha es un misterio."
"Ciudadana, el estampido detiene la vida,
también el estampido abre senderos."

Entonces salí a la calle a preguntar
al científico y al cocinero:
"Señora, si observo el átomo soy más que un dios,
si contemplo el cosmos no valgo un bledo."
"Usuaria, mire, para el corazón y la lengua
mi técnica es paciencia y mucho fuego."

Entonces salí a la calle a preguntar
al filósofo y al misionero:
"Ser, la materia ni se crea ni se destruye,
su ley fundamental es lo eterno."
"Hija, el verbo fue antes del principio
y ahora y luego."

"Customer, you have enough for salt,
but you do not have enough for honey."

Then I went out into the street to ask
the mason and the plumber:
"Madam, the best thing is to pour another ceiling,
although if you add a beam the roof will hold up."
"Aunt, that pipe is still strong,
hurry, buy yourself a new toilet float."

*helpful in reality
of problem
↓
less expensive
solutions*

Then I went out into the street to ask
the teacher and the carpenter:
"Student, one plus one is two.
Two times zero is zero."
"Housewife, varnish adds only shine;
make war with termites before the wood dies."

Then I went out into the street to ask
the farmer and the artilleryman:
"Sister, seeding depends on you,
the harvest is a mystery."
"Citizen, gunshot stops life,
and gunshot also opens paths."

Then I went out into the street to ask
the scientist and the cook.
"Madam, if I observe the atom, I'm more than a god;
if I contemplate the cosmos, I'm not worth a penny."
"Money lender, look, in matters of heart and tongue,
my technique is patience and a hot fire."

Then I went out into the street to ask
the philosopher and the missionary:
"Being, matter is neither created nor destroyed;
its fundamental law is the eternal."
"Daughter, the Word was before the beginning
is now and evermore."

*- their answers
are irrelevant
to complaint-
displacement*

*repetition of form —▷ process of knowledge
- paternalistic figures — diff. level of society -
- they're telling her why she's going about answers in wrong way
- all calling her by social roles (no name)*

Entonces salí a la calle a preguntar
en las oficinas y en los ministerios.
Y llené papeles y redacté autobiografías.
Y conté mi vida desde el fin hasta el comienzo.

Entonces salí a la calle a preguntar
a los niños, a los viejos, a los secretos.

Entonces salí a la calle a preguntar
a la tierra, al mar, al fuego, al cielo.

Entonces salí a la calle a preguntar
por mis manos. Por mis manos. Por mis manos
en el enigma del ser estando y siendo.

Soy yo. La Esposa:
díganme,
si no el culpable, al menos, el primero.
Díganme,
¿por qué contra la lógica aristotélica de mi familia
no formé un clan de pardos ingenuos?
Díganme,
¿dónde está la niña linda
—como sólo saben serlo las niñas—
que se sentaba a soñar en el puerto?
Díganme,
¿dónde está la muchacha confiada
—como sólo saben serlo las muchachas—
que se recostó a nacer contra un pecho?
Díganme,
¿dónde está la mujer segura
—como sólo saben serlo las mujeres—
que abrió los brazos a un niño viejo
de alcoles y rechiflas y monte y monte
y madre y egoísmo y murciélago?
Díganme,
¿dónde está? ¡Tráiganmela a Ella!
porque Ella es la Esposa,

Then I went out into the street to ask
in offices and ministries.
And I filled out papers and edited autobiographies.
I told my life from the end to the beginning.

Then I went out into the street to ask
children, elders, and secret ones.

Then I went out into the street to ask
earth, sea, fire, and sky.

Then I went out into the street to ask
about my hands. About my hands. About my hands
in the enigma of being and existing.

It is I. The Wife:
tell me,
if not the guilty one, at least, the first one.
Tell me,
why against the Aristotelian logic in my family
didn't I create a clan of ingenuous mulattos?
Tell me,
where is the pretty girl
—as only pretty girls know how to be—
who used to sit on the dock and dream?
Tell me,
where is the confident young girl
—as only young girls know how to be—
who leaned against a man's chest to be born?
Tell me,
where is the secure woman
—as only women know how to be—
who opened her arms to an old alcoholic child,
to jeering, to backwardness,
mother, and egotism and bats?
Tell me,
where is she? Bring Her to me!
Because She is the Wife,

la que espantó al miedo,
la que sirvió de escalera,
la que veló estudios y proyectos,
la que engañaron, la defraudada,
la que abandonaron en un aeropuerto,
la que esperó mil noches y una noche
y mil noches y una noche agujerearon los insectos,
la que fue al manicomio,
la que encerraron entre cunas de hueso.
Es Ella la única que puede decirme
quién le manchó las manos de sangre
en este aquelarre de soledad y veneno.

Pero yo soy la Esposa
y sólo tengo preguntas abiertas
y una llave de plomo
                    que no abre, sino cierra.
Antigua llave sin brillo
                    en el fulgor de esta llavera.
La usó mi abuela, y mi madre
y las abuelas de abuela
—la frágil carabalí
                    de la tersa piel morena
y la adusta castellana,
                    rosa fiel, flor marfileña—.
En la recámara de piedra y cristo
y en la choza de engorde y selva,
                              la misma llave,
la misma, que no puede ya cerrar ninguna reja.
Mi vieja llave herrumbrosa
                    en algún rincón que se queja,
en algún rincón que ni grita
                    ni balbucea,
en algún rincón de cristal,
en algún rincón de fetiche y cuentas,
en algún rincón de barro,
en algún rincón de oración y velas,

the one who frightened away fear,
the one who served as staircase,
the one who watched over studies and projects,
the one others cheated, the defrauded one,
the one others abandoned in an airport,
the one who waited a thousand and one nights
and one thousand and one nights while the insects bore through,
the one who went to the insane asylum,
the one who was closed up within cradles of bone.
She's the only one who can tell me
who stained her hands with blood
in this witches' sabbath of loneliness and poison.

But I am the Wife
and I only have open questions
and a lead key
          that does not open, but closes.
Old key, no longer shiny
                    in the light of this holder of the keys.
My grandmother used it, and my mother
and the grandmothers of my grandmother
—fragile Carabalí woman
          of smooth dark skin
and the austere Castilian
          faithful rose, ivory flower—.
In the dressing room of stone and Christ,
and in the jungle hut for fattening cattle,
                    the same key,
the same one, that no longer locks any gate.
My old rusty key
                    in some corner complaining,
in some corner not even screaming
                    nor stammering
in some crystal corner,
in some corner of fetishes and beads,
in some clay corner,
in some corner of prayers and candles,

[handwritten margin notes:]
→ next step for finding answers
historical realm of cuba
diff modes of worship —◦ catholicism + Yoruba
— women have always used key to lock things up — to forget

en algún rincón de la sangre donde hay
cientos de manos carcomidas y muertas.

Soy yo. La Esposa.
Del rincón de la sangre vuelvo.
Allí encontré a mi padre
                              en una tarde de juegos:
que no es mulato, dice,
                              sino gitano de baile flamenco.
Y vamos en un carromato
                              leyendo palmas y dedos.
Y las manos están limpias
                              y se las cuelgo al cuello.

La Señorita Hija
entrando en el baile;
que lo baile, que lo baile;
y si no lo baila
le doy castigo malo;
que la saque, que la saque.
Salga usted, que la quiero ver bailar . . .

Y me saca el Padre
                              y me da la vuelta
y me gira en el humo
                              y me cerca en la siesta.
            En los vapores del ron,
            la niña fue sólo hembra.

"La niña se ahogó en el pozo
entre sapos y culebras"
—gritan por toda la cuadra
Nené Traviesa y Cenicienta—.

Y me saca el Padre
                              y me da la vuelta
y me gira en el humo
                              y me cerca en la siesta.

"Que la traigan en andas
güijes y comadrejas"

in some bloody corner full
of worm-eaten and dead hands.] the real secret

It is I. The Wife.
From the bloody corner I return. → no more distancing
There I found my father
                    in an afternoon of games:
who is not mulatto, he says,
                    but rather a flamenco gypsy dancer.
And we ride in a two-wheeled cart
                    reading palms and fingers.
And my hands are clean
                    and I hang them around his neck.

The Maiden Daughter
entering the dance;
let her dance, let her dance;
and if she doesn't dance
I'll punish her bad;
lead her out to dance, lead her out.
Let her come out, I want to see her dance . . .

— children's poems

And my Father leads me out
                    and he turns me around
and he whirls me in the smoke
                    during the siesta he circles me 'round.
        In vapors of rum,
        the girl was only a maiden.

& "My Papa's waltz"
— Roethke

→ children out playing —
parents "napping"
(having sex)

"The girl drowned in the well
amongst bull frogs and snakes."
Naughty Little Girl and Cinderella
yell all around the block.

also disobeys mandate
↓
neither have mother

And my Father leads me out
                    and he turns me around
and he whirls me in the smoke
                    during the siesta he circles me 'round.

first dancing w/ father at wedding

"Let her be brought on the shoulders
of güijes and weasels,"

— suitors also wanted her to dance (pg 23)

—*el eco, ecoooo, responde*
tiritando en las gavetas—.

Y me saca el Padre
                    y me da la vuelta
y me gira en el humo
                    y me cerca en la siesta.

"La niña es un monigote
y estatua de sal añeja"
—van gritando los portones
de la casa de muñecas—.

Y me saca el Padre
                    y me da la vuelta
y me gira en el humo
                    y me cerca en la siesta.

La suiza se hace un nudo:
horca de saltos perplejas.

Y me saca el Padre
                    y me da la vuelta
y me gira en el humo
                    y me cerca en la siesta.

La niña lleva a la niña
en un carretón de penas.

Y me saca el Padre
                    y me da la vuelta
y me gira en el humo
                    y me cerca en la siesta.

La niña llora a la niña
con llanto de azúcar prieta.

Y me saca el Padre
                    y me da la vuelta

the echo answers, the echooo
shaking from inside the drawers.

And my Father leads me out
                and he turns me around
and he whirls me in the smoke
                        during the siesta he circles me 'round.

"The girl is a ragdoll
and statue of aged salt,"
the large doors
of the dollhouse keep shouting.

And my Father leads me out
                and he turns me around
and he whirls me in the smoke
                        during the siesta he circles me 'round.

The jump rope turns into a knot:
a gallows of perplexed leaps.

And my Father leads me out
                and he turns me around
and he whirls me in the smoke
                        during the siesta he circles me 'round.

The girl leads the girl
in a wagon of sorrows.

And my Father leads me out
                and he turns me around
and he whirls me in the smoke
                        during the siesta he circles me 'round.

The girl cries for the girl
with tears of dark sugar.

And my Father leads me out
                and he turns me around

y me gira en el humo

                y me cerca en la siesta.

¡La niña no tiene niña.
Ay, tarde de incesto y teas!

(UN GALLO DE TERCIOPELO,
UN CANARIO QUE NO VUELA,
UN PECESITO DORMIDO,
UN ESPEJO DE DOS PESETAS.)

La niña ha resucitado
en un charco de vergüenza.

(¡Que no, que no quiero verla!)

Las manos. Las manos, ¿quién puede
lavar mis manos o mis ojos, o mi pelo,
o mis brazos, o mi boca, o mis pulmones,
o mi cerebro? ¿Qué cante jondo,
qué sota de oros, qué rey de bastos,
qué as de copas, qué caballo
de espadas, qué malaventura, qué taconeo,
qué paloma, qué ebbó, qué recogimiento,
qué hombre no dado a luz por mujer,
Padre, podrá exorcizarte el recuerdo?

I am —Ⓓ more active than "It is I"

Soy yo. La Esposa:
Un Nido de paja, tierno.
Tengo la misión del trino . . .
y sólo preparo el vuelo.

Soy yo. La Esposa:
Un Erial bajo los truenos.
Feraz de tierras me sé . . .
pero zafra soy de miedo.

Soy yo. La Esposa:
Forma de templado acero.

and he whirls me in the smoke
               during the siesta he circles me 'round.

The girl has no girl.
Ah, afternoon of incest and flambeaux!   ~~names it~~

(A VELVET ROOSTER.
A CANARY WHO DOES NOT FLY,
A LITTLE FISH ASLEEP,
A TWO-PENCE MIRROR.)

The girl has returned to life
in a puddle of shame.

(But no, I do not want to see her!)

My hands. My hands. Who can
wash my hands or my eyes, or my hair,
or my arms, or my mouth, or my lungs,
or my brains? What soulful song,
what jack of gold, what king of clubs,
what ace of cups, what knight
of spades, what misadventure, what dance,
what pigeon, what ebbó, what gathering,
what power of man, for none of woman born,
Father, could exorcise for you the memory?

It is I. The Wife;
A Nest of straw, tender,
I have the mission of a bird's fury . . .
and I prepare only for flight.

It is I. The Wife:
A Wasteland under the thunder.
Fertile of lands I know myself to be . . .
but I am the harvester of fears.

It is I. The Wife:
Form of tempered steel,

Creí que sería escudo . . .
en yunta llegué al arriero.

Soy yo. La Esposa:
Yacimiento a cielo abierto.
Me soñe rojo rubí . . .
otros me vieron pieza de ébano.

Soy yo. La Esposa:
La Encajera de sueños.
Diseñé un traje de rey . . .
zurcí un jirón harapiento.

Soy yo. La Esposa:
Apetedbí del omiero.
Monja feudal de clausura . . .
Penélope sin Odiseo.

¿Y no vendrá un día alguien a mimarme el gesto?
¿Y no vendrá alguien a decirme que es

> > > *el bodeguero*
> > > *el médico*
> > > *el plomero*
> > > *el albañil*
> > > *el carpintero*
> > > *el maestro*
> > > *el artillero*
> > > *el campesino*
> > > *el cocinero*
> > > *el científico*
> > > *el misionero*
> > > *el filósofo*
> > > *el viejo*
> > > *el niño*
> > > *el secreto?*

¿Y no vendrá alguien del fondo de todos los álguienes
—sobrio y sereno—,

> > *alguien con falo de árbol,*
> > *alguien con ojos de nido nuevo,*
> > *alguien con boca de erial,*

I thought I would be a shield . . .
but I reached the muleteer in a yoke.

It is I. The Wife:
Bedrock open to sky . . .
I dreamt myself a red ruby;
others saw me as a piece of ebony.

It is I. The Wife:
The Keeper of dreams.
I designed a king's robe . . .
I stitched a tattered rag.

It is I. The Wife:
Apetedbí for the omiero.
Feudal cloistered nun . . .
Penelope without Odysseus.   places herself among classics

Triumphant ending

Will someone not arrive someday to indulge me with a gesture?
Will someone not come to tell me he is

> *the shop keeper*
> *the doctor*
> *the plumber*
> *the mason*
> *the carpenter*
> *the teacher*
> *the artilleryman*
> *the peasant*
> *the cook*
> *the scientist*
> *the missionary*
> *the philosopher*
> *the old man*
> *the child*
> *the secret one?*

Will someone not come from the depths of all the someones
—sober and serene—

> *someone with a tree trunk phallus,*
> *someone with eyes of a new nest,*
> *someone with a wasteland mouth,*

alguien con brazos de templado acero,
alguien con voz de encaje,
alguien con pecho de yacimiento,
Señor de un Feudo de Luz,
Vencedor de Sirenas, Güijes y Espectros.
Alguien que sepa ser

cazador y lobo,
azor y presa,
navegante y peregrino,
monje y juglar,
sacerdote y ateo.

Alguien que viva a estar vivo.

Alguien que muera a estar muerto.

Alguien que me lave las manos como un padre feliz,
y me las enjoye luego

con fuego y pasión,
con fuerza y con ruegos.

Alguien que diga:

I am
"Soy yo. El Esposo."
Y comencemos unidos la Cópula del Universo.

La Habana, octubre–noviembre de 1984

someone with arms of tempered steel,
someone with a voice of lace,
someone with a chest to lie on,
Master from a Fiefdom of Light,
Conqueror of Sirens, Güijes and Specters
Someone who knows how to be
        hunter and wolf,
        goshawk and prey,
        sailor and pilgrim,
        monk and minstrel,
        priest and atheist.

someone who can deal with contradictions

Someone who lives to be alive.

→ now she can find a proper husband

Someone who dies to be dead.

Someone who will wash my hands as a happy father would,
and who will adorn them later

↓ reclaiming of sexuality from guilt

                with fire and passion,
                with strength and prayers.

Someone who will say:

more passive

                "It is I. The Husband."
And together we will begin the Copula of the Universe.

Havana, October–November, 1984.

A través del espejo

Escribo todo esto con la melancolía
de quien redacta un documento.

Eliseo Diego

Detrás del espejo
                  todas las reinas discuten su linaje
transitorio:
            consagrado
reverso del gato zarandeado por una niña insolente.
                  Alfil-caballo-alfil
                  —tablero de melón—:
                  la dama perejil
                  mata al peón.
(Ah, escribo todo esto con la melancolía
de quien redacta un documento y traza su destino
a punta y sonrisa de tijeras.)
                  No hay prisa,
                        corta
lenta la oreja sobre la yeguada
como una ceniza en la barbería del hijo pródigo.
                  Y la medida luminosa
                        une
la fibra aventada con el pez y el huracán.
Quien une, separa.   Quien aplaca, incita.
Pero si el pez se lo propusiera
                        sería el mar
o si el huracán quisiera
                        fundaría las islas;
y yo, si insisto, seré yo señoreando sobre el desastre y la
                                    escama.
Sólo que el pez cede a la tentación del anzuelo,
el huracán se empecina en el viento contrario de su furia.
Y en cuanto a mí, termino disputándole a la soledad
                  el remo que clava astuta
      entre dos faros   y un curujey de plastilina.

Through the Looking Glass

I write all this with the melancholy
of one who drafts a document.

Eliseo Diego

Behind the looking glass
all queens debate their ephemeral
lineages:
hallowed
inverse presence of the cat shaken by an impertinent girl.
bishop-knight-bishop
—chess board of melon—:
the parsley queen
kills the pawn.
(Ah, I write this with the melancholy
of one who drafts a document and traces her destiny
using a scissors' point and smile.)
There is no hurry.
Cut
the ear slowly on top of nonsense
like one ash in the barbershop of the prodigal son.
And the luminous measure
unites
the thread strewn to the wind with the fish and the hurricane.
Whoever unites, separates.   Whoever placates, incites.
But if the fish meant to,
it would become the sea,
or if the hurricane wanted to,
it would establish the islands;
and I, if I insist, I will be I, lording it over both the
disaster and the fish scale.
But the fish gives in to the temptation of the hook,
the hurricane insists on the obstinate wind of its fury.
And as for me, I end up challenging loneliness
for the oars that it cunningly plants
between two lighthouses   and weeds made of modeling clay.

No hay prisa,
toda la eternidad
cabe
del canto de la piña   a la alta voz de la jícara,
del cortés abanico   al elegante cirio
con su guayabera de domingo.
No hay prisa,
pongo el dedo sobre mi propia llaga,
macabra mercancía
que contemplo y velo desconsolada hasta que me subaste.
El Anticuario
como una realización de fin de temporada
—compra en remate del polvo y el olvido—.
No hay prisa,
ya me venderán el reloj
de no estar,
de no
es-
tar
más,
con sus tres manecillas marcando la hora de los mameyes:
Una detenida en el comienzo,
otra en el horror
salivoso de la esperanza y todavía quedará una tercera
para la orfandad,   para la viudez,
para el desperdicio de tanto futuro sin mí misma.
No hay prisa,
me evaporo:
la misteriosa cantidad es un ratón disfrazado de grillo,
un oscuro sobresalto, un conocimiento fatal.
Sí, escribo todo esto con la melancolía de quien redacta
un documento,
con la amargura de un cronista social sin corbata,
con toda la tristeza y la lástima de la que soy capaz.
Roe,
roe, corta y roe,
diente y violín,
volatín volatinero

There is no hurry,
all eternity
fits
between the song of the pineapple   and the high voice of the gourd cup,
between the courtesan's fan   and the elegant wax candle
with its Sunday guayabera.
There is no hurry,
I place my finger on my own wound,
                                        deathly merchandise
that I, disconsolate, muse and guard over until I'm raffled off
by the Auctioneer,
as if at the end of the season sale
        —remaindered from dust and forgetfulness.
There is no hurry.
Later, they will sell me the clock
of not being
of not
be-
ing
anymore,
with its three hands tracing the hour of the ripe mameyes.
One has stopped at the beginning,
                        another at the slippery
horror of hope, and there will be yet a third
for orphanhood,   for widowhood,
for the terrible waste of so much future without me, myself.
There is no hurry,
I evaporate:
the mysterious entity is a mouse disguised as a cricket,
a dark surprise, a fatal knowledge.
Yes, I write all this with the melancholy of one who drafts
a document,
with the bitterness of a social chronicler without necktie,
with all the sadness and self-pity of which I am capable.
Gnaw,
gnaw, cut and gnaw,
tooth and violin,
rope-walker, rope-dancer

del cordero, asa tu pernil
con la mecha del candil.
Desde el espejo salta la imagen y busca su espacio,
maúlla negra la imagen del gato. Cristalina y frágil
maúlla.
Y atrás, dándole la espalda al gato del espejo, el gato
que mira dentro y busca su anverso majestuoso:
Rostro de reina y lomo de felino.

mayo de 1988

Nanas del elefante caminante

FRESCO y fragante
va un elefante,
muy elegante
con su turbante.

Mas, pasa un carro,
pisa un guijarro…
y cae en un jarro
lleno de barro.

Y el elefante
—en un instante—
queda chorreante
—atrás y alante.

"Luego me barro
todo este embarro."
Y tan campante
sigue adelante.

roast your leg of lamb
with the wick of an oil lamp.
From the looking glass jumps the image and looks for its space,
the cat's image miaows black. Crystalline and fragile
it miaows.
And behind, turning away from the cat in the mirror, the cat
who looks inside and looks for its majestic reverse presence:
Queen's face and feline back.

May 1988.

Lullaby for an Elephant Out for a Stroll

FRESH and fragrant
strolls an elephant,
very elegant
in his turban.

- another self portrait
- Morejon gets all the attention outside of Cuba; nobody reads Saldaña's major poetry
- elephants never forget

But a cart rumbles
by and he tramples
a pebble and tumbles
into a pot brimful of mud.

The elephant
—all in a flash—
stands dripping, awash
—both foreparts and back.

"Later I'll trouble
with this mud-messy jumble."
And, just as buoyant,
he proceeds to advance.

from Honey Gourd

Nanas del niño-cosmos

Para Esteban Llorach
en la fidelidad del corazón.

Dime,
　¿con qué brizna de espejo,
　con qué granito de barro,
　con qué roce de dedos,
　con qué suspiro de magia,
　con qué huesito de sueño,
　con qué susurro de hormiga,
　con qué frutilla de fuego,
　con qué minucia de polen,
　con qué sorbito de vuelo,
　con qué burbuja de música,
　con qué acorde de eco,
　con qué punto sin fin,
　con qué chispa de tiempo,
　con qué pizca de nada,

　con qué te hice,

　mi niño, mi hijo,
　mi cosmos perfecto?

-most difficult poem to translate

Nanas de mi majadero

Para todos los Vitier,
sobre una guitarra, un verso
y un piano.
Para Cintio y Fina, la gran semilla.

CUANDO te escondes,
　mi majadero,
　el mundo entero
　gira y se vuelve
　atolladero:

La cuna flota

Lullaby for the Child-Cosmos

For Esteban Llorach
in the faithfulness of his heart.

[handwritten: – a little bit like Lewis Carrol' – whimsical]

Tell me,
with what splinter of mirror,
granule of clay,
touch of my finger
or magical sigh,
with what fragment of dream,
whisper of ant,
berry of fire, or iota of pollen,
with what
flight's little sip, what
bubble of music,
what harmony of
echo, point without
end, what spark of time
or jot of nothing,

with what did I create you,

my child, my son,
my consummate cosmos?

Lullaby for My Naughty Child

For all the Vitiers,
above a guitar, a verse
and a piano.
For Cintio and Fina, the great seed.

WHEN you hide,
my naughty child,
the whole world
gyrates, becomes
a morass:

[handwritten: – without this child, she wouldn't be most important Cuban poet who writes for children]

The cradle floats

sobre burbujas,
entre pilotes
de siete agujas.
(El blanco es negro,
el negro, gris;
cada pañuelo
busca nariz.)
El biberón
se va de farra
(a la maruga
nadie la agarra).
El verde coge
color de fresa,
el amarillo
va de cabeza.
Y la tetera
salta a la coja
en la escalera,
con la cotorra.

Cuando te escondes,
mi majadero
el mundo entero
gira y se vuelve
atolladero:
Lavo la sal,
frío un sillón
—qué revoltura,
qué dispersión—,
pelo un culero,
tiendo el fogón,
plancho la leche,
coso un rincón.
De nada sirvo,
soy un error:
—Si ya no hay niño,
¿qué cosa soy?

—Polvo que barre
esta canción.

on bubbles,
among bearing piles
of seven needles.
(White is black,
black, grey;
every handkerchief
hunts for its nose.)
The nursing bottle
goes out on a spree,
(and the rattle?
No one can catch it.)
Green takes
color from strawberry,
Yellow
walks on its head.
And the teapot
leaps and limps
in the stairway,
with the parrot.

When you hide,
my naughty child,
the whole world
gyrates, becomes
a morass.
I wash the salt,
I fry an armchair
—what a scrambling,
what a scattering—
I peel a diaper,
I fold down the stove,
I iron the milk,
I sew a nook.
I'm good for nothing,
I'm all a mistake:
If there is no child,
What thing am I?
—Dust that this song
sweeps up.

Nanas de la desaparecida

Para Analaura, in memoriam,
Hija.

I

VEN, acércate, perdóname,
niña mía, dolorosa
—buscadora silenciosa
de la caricia negada.

¿O hurtas tu huella alada
en aire desconocido
y con él te me has vestido,
harapienta de terror?

Di, ¿dónde hallar tu color?,
¿dónde te olvidas llorando
del juego que estás jugando,
del juego de este dolor?

II

La tierra niega su peso,
la lluvia seca su manto,
el pájaro olvida el canto,
la abeja, su pronta miel.

Grito, espina, frío, hiel
sólo habrá, tan sólo ha habido:
tú no eres, no has nacido,
¿qué más puede suceder?

Huérfana de mi querer,
hija de rara belleza,
reclina tu fiel cabeza
para siempre en soledad.

Mi velamen de bondad,
no te encrespes en mi oleaje,

Lullaby for the Missing Daughter

For Analaura, in memoriam.
Daughter.

I

COME, draw near, forgive me,
my child, my mournful one,
—searching silently
for the caress withheld.

[handwritten note: —child born / still born / — much slower / rhythm than / previous poems]

Or do you withdraw your winged footprints
into nameless air
and have you clothed yourself there
tattered in terror?

Tell me where to discover your coloring?
Where crying, do you become oblivious
to the game you are playing,
the game of this pain?

II

The earth disclaims its weight,
the rain dries its mantle,
the bird forgets its song,
the bee, its store of honey.

[handwritten note: everything loses / what can / make it beautiful]

Only howl, thorn, cold, gall
will be; only these have been:
you are not, have not been born,
what else can occur?

Orphan of my desire,
daughter of rare beauty,
rest your devoted head
forever in loneliness.

My sail of goodness,
do not pitch yourself in my rough sea,

sal vencedora en el viaje,
escapa, alza limpio vuelo;

aunque estoy por ti de duelo,
silenciosa me he de estar;
mas, ten piedad, dame hogar,
allá donde hagas tu cielo.

Tengo sed, abuela

—Tengo sed, abuela.
—Anda, bebe algo fresco.
—Tengo sed, abuela.
—Caza las gotas del viento.
—Tengo sed, abuela.
—El río no está lejos.
—Tengo sed, abuela.
—Eso lo quita un beso.

escape victorious, survive the journey,
flee, rise in unencumbered flight;

although I mourn for you,
I must remain silent;
but, have pity, give me a home,
there, where you make your heaven.

I'm thirsty, Grandmother

—I'm thirsty, Grandmother.
—Go, drink something cool.
—I'm thirsty, Grandmother.
—Look for drops of wind.
—I'm thirsty, Grandmother.
—The river isn't far.
—I'm thirsty, Grandmother.
—A kiss will put an end to that.

La Habana, en el año 50 de mi vida

Mi fiel:

Ahora cierro los ojos y todo es noche: la noche de mi cuerpo. Todo es soledad. Todo es silencio. El pájaro dorado del silencio. Y yo entro en la pajarera del recuerdo.

Pero entro sin memoria, como un soldado que tras largos años regresara a una ciudad por donde alguna vez pasó su caravana—a penas un destello en el diorama de los recuerdos de su propia guerra—ése del olvido generoso de la vanidad salvadora, que confunde rechazos con vitores, derrotas con liberación. Entro descubriendo lo conocido. Sin odios. Sin culpas. Calmadamente, sin entusiasmos ni indiferencias. Sin recuerdos en el recuerdo. Sin nostalgia.

Una ciudad más y un soldado entre miles y una guerra como tantas otras: inútil, perdida ya antes que fuera guerra. . . . Mas aún, antes de que hubiera contrincantes. Nada unió a la ciudad y al soldado, salvo las dos caras de una consigna de tan repetida, olvidada; de tan eterna, obsoleta. Ciudad y soldado fueron enfrentados por el azar, por el juego inconsciente de la fortuna igual que a ti y a mí nos convirtió en agonistas, la casualidad. Nada nos ata. Nada. Ni dolor ni alegría. . . . O tal vez esta libertad es nuestro grillete más oneroso. Quizás somos los esclavos de una ternura que perdimos, tal el soldadito anónimo y su aldheucha: una plaza escondida, el polvo antiguo de un rincón inexistente, un muchachito lloroso y atemorizado. . . . Soy el soldadito que se creyó un héroe, el soldadito con hambre de hazañas que entra en el recuerdo, muerde su pulpa hostil y a dentelladas parte el cuesco donde una ciudad dormida espera.

No, no cierro los ojos, sino que los abro: quiero ver y ver y mirar. Y entro en el recuerdo que me invento con jirones de otros recuerdos que también inventé; con hilachas de ti y de otros cuerpos que reprodujiste: imagen de todas las imágenes superpuestas; reflejo distorsionado del cuerpo que fabrico, ininterrumpidamente, para el espejo de mi recuerdo.

Y entro en el recuerdo tocanco tus pies: los dedos largos, aristocráticos; las uñas transparentes, sus lúnulas en menguante; la planta sensible. Toco

Havana, in the 50th year of my life.

My faithful one:

Now I close my eyes and all is night: the night of my body. All is solitude. All is silence. The golden bird of silence. And I enter the aviary of memory.

bird = sexuality

But I enter without memory . . . like a soldier who after many years returns to a city through which his company once moved—hardly a sparkle in the diorama of recollection of his own war—that generous forgetting of a liberating vanity which confuses rejections with acclaim, defeats with liberation. I enter discovering what is known. Without hatreds. Without faults. Calmly, without enthusiasms or indifference. Without recollections in memory. Without nostalgia.

nicely constructed
transparent.
caged, but visible

Another city and a soldier among thousands, and a war like many others: useless, lost even before it was a war. . . . Even yet, before there were combatants. Nothing united the city and the soldier, except the two faces of a slogan, a slogan so repeated, it is forgotten; so eternal, it is obsolete. City and soldier came face to face by accident, by the unconscious game of fortune, just as it made you and me enemies by chance. Nothing ties us. Nothing. Neither pain nor joy. . . . Or perhaps this freedom is our most burdensome shackle. Maybe we are slaves to a tenderness that we lost, much like the anonymous soldier and his little town: a hidden town square, the ancient dust of a nonexistent corner, a mere lad, tearful and terrified. I am the little soldier who thought himself a hero, the little soldier hungry for exploits who enters into memory, bites its hostile flesh, and gnashing its teeth splits the kernel where a sleeping city waits.

No, I do not close my eyes, rather, I open them: I want to see and see and contemplate. I enter into the memory that I invent for myself with shreds of other memories that I also invented; with threads of you and of other bodies that you fabricated: an image of all the superimposed images: distorted glare of the body that I build for you, uninterrupted, for the mirror of my memory.

one person but also much bigger than that

And I enter into memory touching your feet: the long toes, aristocratic; the transparent toenails, with their half moons, with their sensitive soles.

tus pies—blancos, casi azules—con el revés de mi ojos. Los memorizo: me los llevo para siempre: te dejo trunco, inacabado, como una estatua de mármol corroída por el salitre.

Ha comenzado el saqueo.

Sí, entro en el recuerdo, en cada uno de tus detalles, para que tu recuerdo sea más tú que tú mismo, y que nada quede a la improvisación apresurada de la soledad. . . .

Y entro en el recuerdo aherrojando tus tobillos; cautivos de mis manos los rodeo de cadenas de hierro y sueños para que no escapes. Y, confiada, asciendo por tus piernas, clavo mis uñas, me agarro morosa al saliente de tus rodillas, adivino el entrante de las corvas, escalo hasta los muslos, alcanzo sin prisa las ingles, oteo la lejanía. Escucho tu voz: te veo, niño inválido, arqueado, como una caricatura de Praxisteles. Te llevo en brazos. Estoy contigo en tu cansancio mañanero, cargo tu frustración, tu rabia, tu envidia por las otras piernas que corren, nadan, patinan, se burlan: "¿Dónde va el cojito que mira un fli, que mira un fla?" ¿Hacia dónde fue, entonces, con sus ojos verdisombras pardiverdes traviesos? ¿A dónde fue? ¿De dónde viene, ahora, con la mirada escurridiza enigmática? ¿De dónde viene a dónde irá con su balanceo disimulado y sensual? ¿A dónde va que mira un fli, que mira un fla?

No sé a dónde ibas entonces, pero yo voy ahora a la cadera que ya quedó marcada, asimétrica, deforme. Voy y me froto. Y repto—risco, pedrusco tibio, pico de la blancura—. Voy y la acaricio, la macrío. . . . Pero no tanto que encele a la cintura: fina como la de un artista de baile jondo, casi femenina en la quebradura de la espalda, casi grotesca en el perfil del desnudo. Pero tuya. Tu cintura. Y mis brazos que la rodean: mi abrazo como un cilicio que la ciñe.

Estoy en el ecuador rítmico de tu cuerpo.
Avanzo hasta tu centro.
Arribo a la meta.

Y entro en el recuerdo con los brazos en alto, triunfadora, saludando a todas las mujeres de mi raza que desde las gradas me vitorean. Competí y

I touch your feet—white, almost blue—with the reverse side of my eyes. I memorize them: I take them away with me forever: I leave you cut short, unfinished, like a marble statue corroded by saltpeter.

The plundering has begun.

Yes, I enter into memory, into each of your particulars, so that your memory can be more you than you yourself, and so that nothing may be left to the hasty improvisation of solitude. . . .

And I enter into memory shackling your ankles with my two hands, fettering your ankles with iron and dreams so that you do not escape. And, trusting, I climb your legs, I dig in my nails, slowly, I catch hold of the prominence of your knees, I guess the entrance to the back of your knees, I climb up your thighs, I reach your groin leisurely, I survey the distance. I listen to your voice: I see you, invalid child, arched, like a caricature of Praxiteles. I carry you in my arms. I am with you in your morning tiredness, I carry your frustration, your rage, your envy of other legs which run, swim, skate, mock you: "Where is the cripple going who looks here, looks there?" Which way did he go, then, with his shadow green eyes, with his hazel green mischievous eyes? Where did he go? Whence does he come, now with that shifty, inscrutable look? Where is he coming from? Where will he go with his deceptive and sensual hobble? Where is the cripple going who looks here, looks there?

I do not know where you were going then, but I am going now to the hip that was already marked, asymmetric, deformed. I go and I stroke myself. I slither—cliff, rough, warm stone, point of whiteness—. I go and I caress it, I indulge it. . . . But not so much that I may make your waist jealous: fine like a flamenco dancer, almost feminine in the break of the back, almost grotesque in the profile of nakedness. But yours. Your waist. And my arms that surround it: my caress like a penitential shirt that encircles it.

I am at the rhythmic equator of your body.
I advance as far as your center.
I arrive at my goal.

And I enter into memory with my arms on high, triumphant, greeting all the women of my race who from the stands call me victorious. I competed

gané: tú eres mi trofeo: un efebo eterno: ni niño ni hombre, en la frontera. Un ángel de una sola pluma, larga y plateada.

Y entro en el recuerdo. Pero no eres un ángel, eres el guardián de la serpiente, la serpiente cuelga entre tus piernas. La serpiente se hace flor.

Y entro en el recuerdo. Entro mirando la flor increíble, la flor manida, la flor trina y única. La flor inefable, la flor verdadera. La protegida por un frágil rizo, delicado, prácticamente inexistente.

Yo he visto el loto. Yo conozco el narciso. Yo he gustado del lirio de los manantiales. Pero ninguno es más suave, pero ninguno es más puro que esta flor blanca que yo rozo con mis labios temiendo que se me asuste; que yo recorro con mi lengua cuidando que no se me lastime; que yo mordisqueo con mis dientes procurando que no se me enoje. Esta flor de carne que yo riego con mi saliva encargándome de que no se me vaya a marchitar.

Y tu flor, poco a poco se alza. Lentamente, se alza. Tímidamente, se alza. Se abre su tallo frágil cual girasol traslucido buscando la luz. Flor para caer quebrada por la brisa, para despetalarse con el viento, para desaparecer en el ojo del tornado.

Pero eso será después, cuando yo sea un huracán: ahora, simplemente, se abre. Ahora se asoma al mundo. Ahora me asombra. Ahora me conmueve. Ahora es la ternura. Ahora es mi alegría. Y yo me solazo bajo su cono de sombra: soy la abeja que zumba, revolotea, zumba, pasa por las costillas atormentadas, se detiene en el lunar púrpura que las estigma, rechaza los ijares famélicos, circunvala el ombligo, vuela hasta las tetillas rosas, se posa y liba.

Yo no quiero nada tabú. Yo amo en la desnudez y en la limpieza. En la salud y la totalidad. . . .

Rodomiel todo tú para mi lengua que zigzaguea, depreda, zumba, revolotea, zumba, lame tus nalgas, explora desfiladeros, cavernas, grutas subterráneas, por donde se entraña y siente, también allí, vibrar el pulso sísmico de tu deseo.

and won: you are my trophy: an eternal ephebe: neither child nor man, at the frontier. An angel with a single plume, long and silvery.

And I enter into memory. But you are not an angel, you are the guardian of the serpent, the serpent hangs between your legs. The serpent becomes flower.

And I enter into memory. I enter marveling at the incredible flower, the mellow flower, the tremulous and unique flower. The ineffable flower, the real flower. The one protected by a fragile curl, delicate, almost non-existent.

I have seen the lotus. I know the narcissus. I have tasted of the lilies from the springs. But none is softer, but none is purer than this white flower that I rub with my lips afraid that it will fear me; that I traverse with my tongue careful that it does not get injured; that I bite carefully with my teeth taking care that it does not become annoyed. This flower of flesh that I water with my saliva, making sure that it will not wilt on me.

And your flower, little by little, it rises. Slowly it rises. Timidly, it rises. Its fragile stem opens like a translucent sunflower looking for the light. A flower made to fall broken by the breeze, to be depetalled by the wind, to disappear in the tornado's eye.

But that will be later, when I will be a hurricane: now, it simply opens. Now it peeks out at the world. Now it dazzles me. Now it moves me. Now it is softness. Now it is my joy. And I relax under the cone of its shade: I am the bee that buzzes, flutters, buzzes, passes by the tormented ribs, stops at the purple place that marks them, rejects the famished flanks, encircles the navel, flies as far as the pink nipples, lands and sucks.

I want no taboo. I love in nakedness and cleanliness. In health and in completeness. . . .

Rose honey are you for my tongue that zigzags, plunders, buzzes, whirls, buzzes, licks your buttocks, explores caverns, narrow passes, subterranean grottoes, where it enters and feels also there, the vibrating seismic pulse of your desire.

Y entro en el recuerdo viéndote disfrutar en la secreta e inconfesada sensibilidad hembra del macho. Y te cubro—varona del varón, hembra que posee—. Y te gozo.

En el silencio lleno de presagios, de miedos antiguos, se oye tu gemido nupcial al oído de este güije sordo e implacable. No quiero oírte. No voy a tener piedad de tu derrota y yo sólo quiero asir tu flor, adornarme con ella el pelo, los hombros, la cintura. Yo quiero su eternidad en la tierra pura y viva del fiel de mis entrepiernas.

¡Pero, ay, sólo yo y la ansiedad del monte sabemos lo que dura la efímera vida de una flor!

Y la tuya antes de frutecer se licua entre mis manos, se hace rocío espeso de la noche, espuma cuajada del mar de la noche, leche recién ordeñada de los ubres de la noche. . . .

Y entro en el recuerdo, como un cachorro abandonado. Dime, ¿cómo endurezco el tallo que la sostenía?, ¿cómo renuevo sus jugos vencidos? Dime, ¿qué hago con esta orfandad que deambula por tu plexo, por el rodil de tu pecho, por tu cabello rubio, crespo y ralo? ¿Dime si puedes conmoverte con mi balido?

Y entro en el recuerdo como un gamo perdido y hambriento. Ahora marmullo tu flor, pétalo a pétalo, tu falo, tu glande, tus testículos, y corro, corro, corro, perseguida por una jauría de lobos jadeantes y me protejo en tu barba, para allí limpiarme todo el llanto blanco de la noche, que tu flor ha sido capaz de sufrir por mi orfandad.

Ah, mi muchachito, mi inacabado, mi nonnato, mi inconquistable, mi feo magnífico: eres perfecto en tu avaricia de ti; perfecto en tu egoísmo contigo, que recibe, se enconcha y halla el círculo eterno; perfecto hasta en la altiva incontinencia que me provoca, en la disfrazada indiferencia, en la debilidad de señorito decimonónico. Perfecto . . . para mi gusto, para mi sensualidad, para mi engolosinamiento, sí, perfecto. Pero yo quiero más. Yo lo quiero todo. Yo lo necesito todo . . . .

And I enter into memory seeing you enjoy in the secret and unconfined female sensibility of the male. And I cover you—a man's mannish woman, a female who possesses—. And I enjoy you.

In the silence full of foreboding, of ancient fears, the ear of this deaf and implacable hostile ghost, hears your nuptial moan. I do not want to hear you. I am not going to have pity on your defeat. I only want to assault your flower, adorn my hair with it, my shoulders, my waist. I want its eternity in pure earth and alive in the faith of the innerside of my inner thighs.

But, aye, only I and the anxiety of the hills know the duration of the ephemeral life of a flower!

And yours, before fruiting, liquefies in my hands, turns into thick dew of the night, curdled foam from the sea of night, milk recently drawn from the udders of the night. . . .

And I enter into memory, like an abandoned pup. Tell me, how do I harden the stem that sustained it? How do I renew its vanquished juices? Tell me, what do I do with this orphanhood that promenades on your solar plexus, on the meadow of your chest, on your blond hair, curly and thin? Tell me if you can be moved by my bleating?

And I enter into memory like a lost and hungry buck. Now I whisper to your flower petal by petal, your phallus, your glans, your testicles, and I run, I run, I run, chased by a pack of panting wolves and I protect myself in your beard, so that there I may wipe from myself all of the white tears of the night, that your flower has been capable of suffering because of my orphanhood.

Ah, my young, young man, my unfinished one, my unborn one, my unconquerable one, my magnificent ugly one: you are perfect in the avarice of yourself; perfect in your egotism with yourself, which receives, is uncoiled and finds the eternal circle; perfect even in the haughty incontinence that it provokes in me, in the disguised indifference, in the weaknesses of a nineteenth-century señorito. Perfect . . . for my taste, for my sensuality, for my sweet tooth, yes, perfect. But I want more. I want it all. I must have it all. . . .

[handwritten margin note: stereotypical Cuban male]

Y entro en el recuerdo y quiero más.

Y ahora soy un vampiro.

Quiero la sangre de tu cuello y más. Tu garganta y más. Tu mentón y más. Tus mejillas y más. Tu nariz y más. Las líneas precoces de tus ojos y más. Tus pestañas y más. Tus cejas y más. El entrecejo y más, tu frente y las arrugas injustas de tu frente y más. Tus sienes y más. Tus orejas y más. Tu nuca y más. Quiero tus venas, tus vísceras, tus músculos, tus glándulas, tus humores, tus pensamientos.

Quiero tu pasión.

Y más.

Y entro en mi recuerdo, no con tu pasión, sino con la mía: con la de toda mi vida: con la que nadie provoca ni conquista: la que yo dono y crezco, porque sí, sin lógica aparente, sin aparente motivo. Mi arma secreta contra la vejez: el renuevo cómplice de mi eterna juventud. Óvulo fecundable por el que entro en el recuerdo para besarte la piel que se extiende con la palidez del rayo de luna: toda la luz riela sobre ti. Piel que inmaculada marinea en las clavículas o que se puebla—en los hombros y en la espalda—de grandes islas de pecas, de archipiélagos oscuros, en los que yo voy desembarcando mi boca, bojeándolos con mis pezones, recorriéndolos hasta llegar a la cayería insignificante de los muslos. Piel que se engrifa como un gato albino al roce de las uñas. Piel que crepita como fuego blanco. Piel lavada en lejía. Piel blanqueada con cal. Piel que huele a piel.

Y entro en el recuerdo torturada por el aroma de tu piel. Entro en el recuerdo porque yo estaría perdida si no existiera tu olor. La noche entera sería cualquier instante, si no estuviera llena de tu olor. Tu cuerpo sería mi enemigo, si no exhalara tu olor. Mi vigilia se convertiría en una pesadilla si yo no velara tu olor. Soy un animal de presa que te rastrea para cobrar la pieza de tu olor.

Y doy con ella. Aspiro y compruebo que el pájaro de mi hambre es tu aliento.

And I enter into memory and I want more.

Now I am a vampire.

I want the blood from your neck and more. Your throat and more. Your chin and more. Your cheeks and more. Your nose and more. The precocious lines of your eyes and more. Your eyelashes and more. Your eyebrows and more. The space between them and more, your forehead and its unjust wrinkles and more. Your temples and more. Your ears and more. The nape of your neck and more. I want your veins, your viscera, your muscles, your glands, your humors, your thoughts.

I want your passion.

And more.

And I enter into my memory, not with your passion, but with mine: with the one from my entire life: with the one that no one provokes or conquers: the one that I bequeath and grow, *because*—no apparent logic, no apparent motive. My secret weapon against old age: the renewed accomplice of my eternal youth. Fecund ovum through which I enter into memory in order to kiss the skin that stretches out like a ray of the moon: all light glimmers on you. Skin that because immaculate, navigates on your collar bones or populates itself—on your shoulders and on your back—of great islands of freckles, of dark archipelagos, on which I go disembarking my mouth, sailing around them with my nipples, traversing through them until I arrive at the insignificant keys of your thighs. A skin that stands on end like an albino cat at a nail scratch. A skin that crackles like white fire. A skin washed in bleach. A skin whitened with lime. A skin that smells of skin.

And I enter into memory tortured by the aroma of your skin. I enter into memory because I would be lost if your smell did not exist. The entire night would be any instant, if it were not filled with your odor. Your body would be my enemy, if it did not exhale your odor. My vigil would turn into a nightmare if I did not keep watch over your odor. I am an animal of prey that tracks you to retrieve the quarry of your odor.

And I arrive at it. I inhale and verify that the bird of my hunger is your breath.

Escucha, si algún día yo me muriera—que lo dudo—rescátame de la tierra. Sopla sobre el vacío de mis oquedades: oréalas. Revíveme. Mata a la muerte con tu aliento para que la vida pueda cosernos puntada a puntada. Eternamente unido a mí, boca a boca.

Y entro en el recuerdo convencida que la eternidad de tu boca es el camino de las especies. Yo juro descubrir el nuevo mundo de tu boca. Para conquistarlo, para invadirlo, para colonizarlo. A nadie más darás esa boca porque yo soy su dueña, porque si quiero la borro con mi beso, porque si quiero la rehago con mi beso, porque si no la beso, no existe. Tu boca no existe fuera de mi beso. . . . Renuncio a todo, menos a tu boca. Lo olvido todo, menos tu boca. Te lo perdono todo, menos tu boca.

Ahora que es mía, odio tu verga de flor efímera y tu cuello de gestos ambiguos y tu color. Tu boca olorosa, líquida, espesa, sólida, roja, exacta, suave, pedigüeña, dadora, todo lo anula, todo lo transforma. . . . Yo necesito que me trague, que sea casta, que sea obscena, que se muera, que jadee, que no se sienta, que se calle, que grite, que muerda, que acaricie, que sea grosera, que sea ingenua, que me chupe, que me frote, que me lama, que me apriete, que me ronche, que me suelte, que me geste, que me abuse, que me obligue, que me venza, que me pida, que me suplique, que se me muera. . . .

Y si por gastada en su oficio ya no tuvieras boca con que venir a mí, entonces yo entraré en el recuerdo de tu madre y entraré en el recuerdo de tu padre y buscaré la cópula en la que te engendraron y entraré en la cópula en la que te engendraron y los obligaré a que vuelvan a hacerte la boca.

Y a esa nueva boca, la tocaré con el pulpejo de mis dedos para que se entreabra y proteste como sacudida por una tormenta de mil rayos, igual que hago con ésta y como con ésta cerraré los ojos y la recorreré con lengua, dientes, pelvis, clítoris, y la mojaré del aceite de mi vagina y la haré tragarse mi orín, mi sudor, mis palabras, mi color, porque ella lo puede todo, ella es el antídoto de todos los venenos y todas las injusticias, ella puede desahalajar a los poderosos, excarcelar a los inocentes, catequizar a los ateos, desbautizar a los apóstoles, desembrujar los aquelarres, legitimizar el demonio, o ser Dios.

Listen, if some day I should die—which I doubt—rescue me from the earth. Breathe on the void of my cavities: set them out to dry. Revive me. Kill death with your breathing so that life may sew us stitch by stitch. Eternally united to me, mouth to mouth.

And I enter into memory convin'ced that the eternity of your mouth is the path to the species. I pledge to discover the new world of your mouth. To conquer it, to invade it, to colonize it. To no one will you give this mouth, to no one because I am its owner, because if I want I erase it with my kiss, because if I want I remake it with my kiss, because if I do not kiss it, it does not exist. Your mouth does not exist outside my kiss. . . . I renounce everything, except your mouth. I forget everything, except your mouth. I forgive you everything, except your mouth.

Now that it is mine, I hate the ephemeral flower of your phallus and your neck of ambiguous gestures and your color. Your odorous mouth, liquid, thick, red, exact, soft, importunate, giving; it annuls everything, it transforms everything. . . . And if I need it to swallow me, let it be chaste, let it be obscene, let it die, let it pant, let it not be felt, let it be still, let it cry, let it bite, let it caress, let it be vulgar, let it be naive, let it suck me, let it rub me, let it lick me, let it squeeze me, let it crunch me, let it release me, let it gestate me, let it abuse me, let it oblige me, let it vanquish me, let it ask me, let it beg me, let it die for me. . . .

And if exhausted in your calling you no longer had a mouth with which to come to me, then I would enter into the memory of your mother and I would find the memory of your father and I would look for the coupling in which they engendered you and I would enter into the coupling in which they engendered you and I would oblige them to make your mouth once more.

And this new mouth I will touch with the soft skin of my fingers so that it may half open and protest as if shaken by a storm of a thousand lightnings, just as I do with this one and as with this one I will close my eyes and I will traverse its tongue, teeth, pelvis, clitoris, and I will wet it with the oil of my vagina and I will make it swallow my urine, my perspiration, my words, my color, because it can do it all, it is the antidote of all the venoms and all the injustices, it can clip the wings of the powerful, it can spring the innocents from prison, catechize the atheist, unbaptize the apostles, exorcise the witches' Sabbaths, legitimize the devil, or be God.

Ella puede ser más que Dios.

Tu boca es la tierra, la tierra cansada y perezosa, la tierra entera, plena cuando se tumba en el horizonte, y hay en tu boca la infinitud del nacimiento y la muerte del Sol.

Y yo soy el Sol.

Yo esplendo sobre ti y te ilumino para que la noche sea la serpiente de fuego del reino inacabado de los dioses.

Y entro en el recuerdo porque sólo los mitos tienen el don de lo inmarcesible. Yo entro en el recuerdo para compartir contigo el privilegio de amar. Yo entro en el recuerdo para enseñarte la humildad de amar. Yo entro en el recuerdo para que aprendas la generosidad de amar.

Amar con todos los cuerpos escondidos del cuerpo
amarte en la carne del espíritu
o en el espíritu de la carne
y en ninguno de los dos
y en los dos sin diferencia.

Y entro en el recuerdo temblando, desnuda y enjoyada de lágrimas, para que tú también puedas desnudarte y llorar.

Es nuestra última oportunidad, el último acto de piedad que se nos concede.

Y entro en el recuerdo buscando tus manos, la sapiencia de ciego de tus manos, la delicadeza de orfebre de tus manos, entro para que me saquees como yo te saqueo, para que me robes como yo te robo, para que me profanes, como yo te profano.

Entro para ser más yo que yo misma en el calco de sangre de mi memoria.
Te pongo las manos para que seas un hombre.
Y los brazos para que las sostengan
y el pozo de las axilas donde se amansa tu olor a agua brava.

Y entro en el recuerdo a pesar de tu flor mustia, a despecho de tu

It can be more than God.

Your mouth is the earth, the tired and lazy earth, the entire earth, full, when it lies down on the horizon, and there is in your mouth the infinity of the birth and death of the Sun.

I am the Sun.   *Whitman*

I shed splendor over you and I illuminate you so that night may become the fire serpent of the unfinished kingdom of the gods.

And I enter into memory because only myths have the gift of that which is unwithering. I enter into memory to share with you the privilege of loving. I enter into memory to teach you the humility of loving. I enter into memory so that you may learn the generosity of loving.

Loving with all the bodies hidden from the body
loving you in the flesh of the spirit
or in the spirit of the flesh
or in neither one of them
and in both without difference.

And I enter into memory shaking, naked and jeweled with tears, so that you also may be able to become naked and to cry.

This is our last chance, the last act of pity that is given to us.

And I enter into memory looking for your hands, the blind person's wisdom of your hands, the goldsmith's fineness of your hands, I enter so that you may plunder me as I plunder you, so that you may steal me as I steal you, so that you may profane me as I profane you.

I enter to be more me than I myself in the tracing of blood of my memory.
I place your hands so that you may be a man.
And the arms so that they sustain them
and the well of the armpits where your odor of rough waters is pacified.

convalescencia indolente de amante, en contra de la pesadez de tus párpados, a contrapelo de la incompetencia lánguida, porque yo confío al menos en la cortesía de tus manos: tus manos de artesano, de hidromiel, de ambrosía, de vino, de asado, de romería, para mi gula insaciable de labriega.

Y entro en el recuerdo y hago que tus manos entren en la fiesta que es mía y tuya. Y entro en el recuerdo y tus manos recorren mis pies de cañandonga, mis calcañales cachazudos: mis pies vulgares. Y mis tobillos montunos y mis piernas de ceiba suntuosa, y mis curvas de azúcar cruda, y mis muslos de jutía conga, y mis nalgas de turrón de caimito y mi espalda agónica, y mi pecho de trapiche, y mis pulmones envejecidos, y mis bronquios de yute agujereado, y mis hombros de raspadura, y mi nuca de palma de corojo, y mis orejas de melado, y mi pelo de yagruma, y mi frente preñada de aparecidos y espectros, y mis ojos equivocados, y mi nariz de sijú platanero, y mi boca de mamey, y mi garganta de tabaco salvaje, y mis caderas de cazuela freidora, y mi vientre de calabaza panuda, y mi cintura de trapo multicolor, y mi ombligo de güira cimarrona, y el triángulo de las prestidigitaciones y el vello maniguero, y el reverso de la concha hacendosa con su perla negra e iridiscente, y la crisma sápida en su crismero de bronce y mis senos de miel, canela y anís.

Y tus manos recorren la unicidad repetida de mis senos.
Y tus manos recorren la parda ingenuidad de mis senos.
Y tus manos recorren simplemente mis senos.
Y tocan.
Palpan.
Rozan.
Ungulan.
Y soy un arpa pulsada que vibra, un concierto de cuerdas que se duele, un danzón gregoriano, una rumba mística, un guaguancó. Soy la nota inaudible de la música de las esferas.

Y tus manos y tu boca, y tu olor, y tu piel, y tus huesos, y tus músculos, y tu sangre, y tus humores, y tu flor muerta y resucitada, y tu cuerpo todo descubren lo que es el sufrimiento, la agonía de la entrega que se enquista y enemiga, del ser ante un cuerpo que escapa; descubren mi cuerpo, este cuerpo gilvo que es el cuerpo del destino, el de las premoniciones, el de la fatalidad. . . .

I enter into memory in spite of your musty flower, in defiance of your indolent lover's convalescence, opposed to the heaviness of your lids, against the grain of languid incompetence, because at least I trust the courtesy of your hands: your hands of an artisan, of mead, of ambrosia, of wine, of roast meat, of festival, for my insatiable farm laborer's appetite.

And I enter into memory and make your hands enter into the feast that is mine and yours. And I enter into memory and your hands traverse my Angolan sugar cane feet, my sluggish heels: my ordinary feet. And my untamed ankles and my sumptuous silk-cotton tree legs, and my crude sugar curves, and my Conga jutía thighs, and my star apple nougat buttocks and my painful back, and my sugar mill breasts, and my worn out lungs, and my gunnysack bronchia, and my raw sugar shoulders, and my nape of cohune palm, and my thick cane syrup ears, and my trumpetwood hair, and my forehead pregnant with specters and apparitions, and my mistaken eyes, and my banana tree gnome owl nose, and my mamey mouth, and my wild tobacco throat, and my frying pan hips, and my bread fruit belly, and my multicolored rag waist, and my runaway calabash bellybutton, and the triangle of prestidigitation and jungle hair, and the reverse of the diligent conch shell with its black and iridescent pearl, and the savory consecrated oil in its bronze oil maker and my breasts of honey and cinnamon and anise.

And your hands traverse the repeated unison of my breasts.
And your hands traverse the brown naiveté of my breasts.
And your hands simply traverse my breasts.
And they touch.
They feel.
Scrape.
Ungulate.
And I am a pulsating harp that vibrates, a painful concert of chords, a Gregorian danzón, a mystic rumba, a guaguancó. I am the inaudible note of the music of the spheres.

And your hands and your mouth, and your smell, and your skin, and your bones and your muscles, and your blood, and your humors, and your dead and resurrected flower, and your whole body discover what suffering is, the agony of surrender of a being that infolds like a cyst, like

Al fin descubres lo que es hambre.
Y tus manos buscan mis manos.
Y tus manos encuentran mis manos.

Y entro en el recuerdo unidas mis manos a las tuyas como quien ora.
Entro repitiendo la plegaria del eco. Entro en la misa de la pareja.

Y entro en el recuerdo oficiando con leche de tamarindo sacralizada; con pezón de champola y ralladura de níspero. Y mamas plenitud y vacío, turgencia y placidez. Y grito. Y gimo. Y gimes y gritas. Y mariposa y puta y mi hembra. Y ven. Y entra. Y carne de mi carne. Y sangre de mi sangre. Y sudor de mi sudor. Y saliva de mi saliva. Y poco o nada importan mi edad, o la fealdad o belleza de mi rostro para dar gracias al azar y a la rueda cósmica, porque entre miríadas y miríadas de combinaciones hizo posible que yo fuera una mujer y que tú fueras un hombre y que nos encontráramos en el momento exacto, en el instante justo y, así, uno encima del otro así y fuera del otro así y dentro del otro, así recién inventados, así recién expulsados de todos los edenes, así girando desde el caos hasta la eternidad así girando así blanco y negro así girando así monstruo bicéfalo así girando así uniéndose, así, girando, así, suspendido, así girando así libres así girando así cayendo así girando así flotando así girando así energía así girando así yéndonos así girando así viniéndonos así viniéndonos así viniéndonos así así así así así así. Ya. Una y otra vez. Ya. Así. Ya. Viniéndonos. Ya. Así ya así ya así una y otra vez ya ya ya. . . . Hasta la paz. . . . ¡Ya!
Ya.

Y entro en el recuerdo y es la paz.
Y salgo del recuerdo y es la paz.

Han muerto los lobos del pecho. Se apaciguó el aullido de las piedras. Los ojos del pavo real se petrificaron. Es la paz. Al fin es la paz.

an enemy, before a body that escapes; they discover my body, this honey-colored body that is the body of destiny, of premonitions, of fatality. . . .
Finally you discover what hunger is.
And your hands look for my hands.
And your hands find my hands.

And I enter into memory with my hands held together with your hands as if praying. I enter repeating the supplication of echo. I enter in the mass of the couple.

I enter into memory officiating with sacerdotal tamarind milk; with a nipple of custard-apple and gratings of medlar. And you suck plenitude and emptiness, pomposity and serenity. I scream. I groan. And you scream and groan. And butterfly and whore and my woman. And come. And enter. And flesh of my flesh. And blood of my blood. And sweat of my sweat. And spit of my spit. And little it matters my age, or my ugliness or the beauty of my countenance in order to give grace a chance and the cosmic circle, because among myriads and myriads of combinations it was possible that I be a woman and that you be a man and that we meet at the exact moment, at the precise instant and, yes, one on top of the other, yes, and outside of the other, yes, inside each other, yes, recently invented, yes, recently expelled from all Edens, yes, spinning from chaos to eternity, yes, spinning, yes, black and white, yes, spinning, yes, two-headed monster, yes, spinning, yes, becoming one, yes, spinning, yes, suspended, yes, spinning, yes, free, yes, spinning, yes, falling, yes, spinning, yes, floating, yes, spinning, yes, energy, yes, spinning, yes, going, yes, spinning, yes, coming, yes, coming, yes, coming, yes, yes, yes, yes, yes, yes. Enough. Once and once more. Enough. Yes. Enough. Coming. Enough. Yes, enough, yes, enough, yes, once and again, enough, enough, enough. . . . Until peace. . . . Enough!
Enough.

And I enter into memory and it is peace.
And I leave memory and it is peace.

The wolves of the breast have died. The howling of the stones have found

Y entro en el recuerdo de ayer para atravesar como el soldadito la última calle del pueblo. Terminó el peligro. Un mundo signa y ejecuta la luz de las palabras. El espejo emigra su revés. Es el recuerdo de antes del comienzo. La suerte está echada.

Quienquiera que seas, quienquiera que hayas sido, quienquiera que puedas llegar a ser, no eres ahora para mí más que un fastasma del cuerpo reencarnado en mi soledad, cuerpo gemelo a mi sombra del que los dioses se sirven y con el que me retan en el enigma de esta noche eterna, la noche en que imagino tu sueño. . . . Cuando todo es oscuridad y yo entro en mi propio recuerdo del recuerdo.

Excilia

peace. The eyes of the peacock were petrified. It is peace. Finally it is peace.

And I enter into memory of yesterday to cross, like the little soldier, the last street of the town. Danger is over. The world signs and executes the light of words. The mirror migrates to its other side. It is the memory prior to the beginning. The die is cast.

Whoever you may be, whoever you may have been, whoever you may become, you are for me nothing more than a specter of the reincarnated body in my solitude, twin body to my shadow, the kind that the gods serve themselves and with which they challenge me in the enigma of this eternal night, the night in which I imagine your dream. . . . When all is darkness and I enter into my own memory of memory.

Excilia

- use of memory
- food/domesticity metaphors
- Cuban nature images (sugar, breadfruit, etc)

- Repetition -

Mi Nombre

(Antielegía Familiar)

A Nicolás Guillén
El apellido entero.
A mi abuela Ana Excilia,
suyo Mi nombre.

(. . .) me dijeron mi nombre. Un santo y seña
para poder hablar con las estrellas.

Nicolás Guillén

Adiós, boca del sueño sin oficio decoroso
realidad
       en el sitio justamente ganado.
Ejerzo otro idioma. Convoco otra dimensión.
Indago
por esta sangre
de ahora, y aquí,
     por esta piel
a trechos
manchada y áspera,
a trechos
fina como un madrigal
o
el suspiro de una niña.
Me camino
      en todo lo que soy,
        o
      que no fui,
en lo que dejaré de ser mañana.

Los recuerdos levantan la mano como colegiales:
                  Al pase de lista
sólo del preferido no hay respuesta.
El ojo insolente,
      ¿dónde se oculta?

My Name
(A Family Anti-Elegy)

To Nicolás Guillén
The whole last name.
To my grandmother Ana Excilia
hers My name.

(. . .) I have been told my name. A password
that I might speak with the stars.

Nicolás Guillén

Good-bye, mouth of the dream without a decorous trade,
reality
      in its place justly gained.
I take up another language. I call forth another dimension.
I investigate
on behalf of this blood
of now, and here,
     of this skin
at times
stained and rough,
at times
refined as a madrigal
or
as a young girl's sigh.
I travel
       into all that I am,
          or
         never was,
or will stop being tomorrow.

Memories raise their hands like schoolchildren:
                            At the roll call
only the teacher's pet does not answer.
The insolent eye,
          where is it hiding?

¿Dónde, la voz rajada y hueca?
El sinsonte temeroso del pecho.
                              ¿Dónde?
¿Dónde está el que soy? ¿Qué olvido me malcría y tutela?

En el fatal vaho de julio se dan cita la guajirita y el proxeneta:
dos cuerpos se presentan
                              y otro surge.
El río crece en el vientre del pez. Se hace garra de león.
Error
        la más bochornosa tarde de agosto
de este siglo nacido bajo la charanga
                              y la Enmienda.
No soy yo.
                No he nacido:
Sin amor nada se engendra.
Y si no soy,
                ¿quién se prende
al pecho fláccido y seco de amargura?
¿Quién espía al Pájaro Azul?
¿A quién le detienen el tiempo en un cartón?
Todo el asombro en la mirada.
Todo el deslumbramiento del Sol.
Y todos los mundos girando sobre su cabeza.

No hay tiempo que perder:
                              pero me pierdo.
No doy conmigo entre las arecas. Me busco
en el hormiguero del patio,
ante los canteros de las adelfas,
bajo el galán de noche,
sobre el aferramiento de la hiedra.
Me llamo por mi nombre
                para acompañarme
gozándome en la idea de que alguien me encuentra.

La respuesta definitiva se halla tras los ojos de vidrio de la
                              última muñeca.

Where is the voice cracked and hollow?
The breast's trembling mocking bird.
                                    Where?
Where is the one that I am? What obliviousness indulges and
    protects me?

father ?

In the deadly vapor of July the country girl and the pimp set a date:
two bodies introduce themselves
                        and another one rises up.
The river grows in the belly of the fish. It becomes the lion's claw.
A mistake
        the sultriest afternoon in August
of this century born under the fanfare
                        and the Amendment.
I am not I.
        I have not been born:
Without love nothing is begotten.
And if I am not,
            who clings
to the breast flaccid and dry from bitterness?
Who spies on the Azure Bird?
For whom is time being held in a box?
All amazement is in the gaze.
All the brilliance of the Sun.
And all worlds turn above his head.

There is no time to lose:
                but I get lost.
I cannot find myself among the palm trees. I look for myself
in the backyard anthill,
before the tubs of oleander,
under the galán de noche,
in the fierce grip of the ivy.
I call myself by my name
                to keep myself company
relishing the idea that someone may find me.

looking for herself

The final answer lies behind the glass eyes of the
                        last doll.

No es por nobleza que no hurgo en el misterio.
No es por piedad.
No es por amor.
                    Sino por miedo.
Todos tenemos miedo:
                    en la casa
semejamos figuras de un ballet grotesco,
en puntillas
            y con el dedo temeroso
                            estrangulando los besos.
En la casa todos tenemos miedo.
Aunque sólo yo arrostre el crimen de burlarme de su cerco:
Cimarrona de los parques,
                    apalencada en el colegio
con mi guámpara de risa
                y mi garabato nuevo:
sin tierra en mi propia tierra:
huyendo cada día del bocabajo
                    y el cepo.
Y para colmo sin el consuelo
                    de los ángeles,
        sin la piedad
                    de los ángeles.
Porque en el aire del trópico los ángeles no contestan.

Mi casa es la primera parada del infierno:
El círculo de los cuchillos y radionovelas.
Entre los ayes de los condenados
                            y el teléfono
esperando una voz,
        el ojo mágico del amo
ordena las rondas de la abuela y la madre
tomadas de las manos
                para la eternidad completa.
Mi madre y la madre de mi padre.
                    Y yo en el centro.
Giran y ruedan.
                    Y yo en el centro.
Gimen y sufren.

Not because of nobility do I not poke at mystery.
Not because of piety.
Not because of love.
                    But because of fear.   → house and house
We are all afraid: as place of
                    in the house   fear
we act like figures in a grotesque ballet,
on tip toe
            and with fearful finger
                            strangling kisses.
In the house we are all afraid.
Although it is I only who defies the crime by mocking its boundaries:
A fugitive slave of the parks,
                            hiding out at school
with laughter, my small machete,
                    and my new scrawl:
without land in my own land:
fleeing each day from the facedown beating   like a runaway
                    and caning.   slave
And to top it all, without the consolation
                            of angels,
            without the pity
                            of angels.
Because in tropic air angels do not answer.

My house is hell's first stop:
A circle of knives and soap operas.
Between the sighs of the condemned
                            and the telephone
waiting for a voice,
        the magical eye of the master
orders the rounds of the grandmother and the mother
holding hands
            for all eternity.
My mother and my father's mother.   like the
                    And I at the center.   rhythm in
                                                     "wife's monologue"
They circle and wheel.
                    And I at the center.   and father
                                                     turning her around
They howl and endure.

Y yo en el centro.
Todos se asoman. Todos las miran.

Y yo en el centro.
¿Dónde buscar cerrajero para esta reja?
¿En qué sitio me alzo o me hundo

a pleno pulmón,
a plena branquia,
a plena libertad
de ser y no morirme?

No en este cuerpo humano.
Y quien no soy se sueña

estrella
o planta
o piedra sensitiva,
mientras

el asma riela por el pecho,
hace crecer las costillas,
atenúa el paso,
dilata las pupilas,
mancha las uñas,
salta en el vientre.
Exorciza.

Enemiga y gemela
también está aquí
con mi madre y la madre de mi padre
y con todos los que giran en la ronda
donde estoy siempre

en el centro
ebria de gritos y maldiciones, suplicando
lo que a los otros sobra:

un trago noble y silencioso de aire
que calme el ulular que llevo dentro.
Nunca
detuvieron la ronda. No a mí
vistieron de blanco

o

limpiaron la piel hasta la transparencia: Mármol
en el sitio de las arterias. Agua

And I at the center.
Everyone peers out. Everyone watches them.
And I at the center.
Where do I look for a lock for this iron grate?
In what place do I rise up or sink down

with full lungs,
with open bronchia,
with the full freedom

of being and not dying?

Not in this human body.

And the one I am not dreams herself

star

or plant

or sensitive stone,

while

asthma glistens through the chest,
swells the rib cage,
slows the foot,
dilates the pupils,
stains the nails,
leaps in the belly.
Exorcises.

Enemy and twin

she's also here

with my mother and my father's mother
and with all who circle in the rounds
where I am always

at the center

drunk with screams and curses, asking for
what others have in excess:

a gulp of air, noble and quiet

to calm the howl I hold inside.
They never
    stopped the circle. No they never
dressed me in white

                or

scrubbed my skin to transparency: Alabaster
in place of arteries. Water

en el curso de la sangre. Palomas
donde hay venas.

De todo soy culpable y lo acepto.
La que no soy—pero me usurpa por costumbre y miedo—
muerde
                la sofisticación del pan
            como una caricia:
Tritura la serpiente.
           Deglute la espada.
              Abre las cancelas prohibidas:
Dios dentro de mi cuerpo de 10 años.
Ah, vanidad de vanidades, vanagloria de la teofagia;
ni mi madre ni la madre de mi padre pudieron devorar
un dios completo, redondo, blanco, insonoro.
No soy yo—pero qué bien lo disimulo bajo la sonrisa tierna—
quien ahora se sienta,
        no a la diestra,
              ni a la siniestra.
          Sino en el centro:
          En el trono de oropel y latas de conservas
dictando el futuro de su raza por los siglos de los siglos.
Y escoge salvarte, Ana Excilia Bregante,
          mulata cariciosa de Atarés,
          ama de las naranjas,
          dueña del coral y el canistel,
          señora del flan de calabaza,
          abuela y mártir,
mientras el país se desgaja
            en bombas y muertos.
Te salvo
       y salvo mi nombre del olvido y del infierno,
hoy,
      8 de diciembre 1956.
No lo supiste nunca:
        ni entonces
          ni después
en aquel hospital donde repetías:

in the course of blood. Doves
for veins.

Of everything I am guilty and I accept that.
The one that I am not—but who usurps me by habit and fear—
bites
                              the sophistication of the bread
                       like a caress:
Grinds the serpent.
                       Swallows the sword whole.
                              Opens the forbidden iron grates.
God inside my 10-year-old body.
Oh, vanity of vanities, conceit of teophagy;
neither my mother nor my father's mother could devour
an entire god, round, white, insonorous.
It is not I—but how well I feign it under a tender smile—
who now sits,
              not on the right
                              nor on the left.
                       But in the center:
       On the throne made with tinsel and tins of jam
dictating the future of her race for ever and ever.
And she chooses to save you, Ana Excilia Bregante,
                       caressive mulatta from Atarés,
                       mistress of oranges,
                       owner of coral and canistel,
                       mistress of pumpkin custard,
                       grandmother and martyr
while the country is torn
                       by bomb shells and corpses.
I save you
              and I save my name from oblivion and hell,
today,
       the 8th of December, 1956.
You never guessed:
              not then
                       nor afterward
in that hospital where you would repeat:

Me tocó perder.

Como si hubieras jugado a la brisca 62 años
con la vida
segura de que a fuerza de paciencia
                            le ganarías la partida.
No lo supiste nunca, Ana Excilia.
Ni entonces
            ni antes del después,
cuando la casa dejó de ser el reino de los almíbares
para convertirse en las ruinas
                            del tamarindo:
ácidas las paredes y tus ojos hinchados detrás
de los espejuelos oscuros. Lágrimas
de ladrillo y cemento, edificios enteros
                                    de amargura,
desahuciada
                por tus inquilinos
                        y con el enemigo en la casa,
                                    el enemigo
que te salva y te ama.
No sólo entonces
            o después.
                        Sino ahora
cuando bajamos por La Víbora hasta el corazón mendicante de
        Lawton.
                                    El enemigo
confirmado por la sortija episcopal
                        y el asentimiento
de los pasionistas,
                apasionados caballeros de la misa
                                    y la mesa.
Desde las agujas de gótico marginal a los baches de San Anastasio,
vamos,
        trinidad de mujeres sin hombre,
misterio de tres cuerpos
                        y un solo crimen,
dogma inefable de la soledad,
tú
        y la mujer de tu hijo.

It's my turn to lose.

As if you had played brisca for 62 years
with your life
sure that by sheer force of patience
                                you would win.
You never knew, Ana Excilia.
Not then,
        not before the afterward,
when the house stopped being the kingdom of fruit preserves
to become the ruins
                of the tamarind:
the walls acid and your eyes swollen behind
dark lenses. Tears
of brick and cement, whole buildings
                        of bitterness,
abandoned
            by her tenants
                    and with the enemy at home,
                                    the enemy
who saves and loves you.
Not then only
        or afterward.
                    But now
when we go down through La Víbora as far as Lawton's
        begging heart.
                            The enemy
confirmed by the Episcopal ring
                        and the throne
of the blest,
            passionate gentlemen of the mass
                            and the table.
From the spires of the near Gothic to the potholes of San Anastasio,
we go.
        A trinity of women without men,
mystery of three bodies
                    and a single crime,
ineffable dogma of loneliness,
you
        and your son's wife.

                                        Y yo en el centro:
                                              El enemigo
purificado y concebido:
                        Madre de todos los futuros mesías,
                        esposa de los múltiples Pepes carpinteros,
                        amante ingenua de cada Gabriel que le diga:
"Llena eres de gracia,
bendito sea tu vientre,
no hay espacio bastante para que lo llene la paloma,
no hay tierra suficiente para sembrar una rosa."

Y el fruto de la niña estalla en sangre y algodones,
salpica a su paso toda la casa,
riega la rosa,
alimenta a la paloma
                para que emigren ave y flor
en busca de su exacta dimensión.
La primera semilla anuncia la primavera.

No para mí:
                Yo habito en un desierto de azúcares turbinadas.
A través de la mulatez del melado
                                oteo un cuerpo:
me regodeo
                en el cañaveral inédito del pubis,
                en el penacho de la cabeza,
                en el desmoche de las axilas,
                en el breve trapiche de los pechos,
                en las piernas espesas,
                en el tacho de bronce del ombligo,
                en la centrífuga de los ojos,
                en los dientes refinos.

Yo sólo sé oírme la sangre
                        y la angustia
ante la belleza inevitable del niño de nácar
y turquesa,
el bibelot
frente al que boquiabierta estira la mano

And I at the center:
The enemy
purified and conceived:
Mother of all future messiahs,
wife of the multiple carpenter Joes,
innocent lover of any Gabriel who tells her:
"Full of grace,
blessed be thy womb,
there is not enough space for the dove,
there is not enough space to cultivate a rose."

And the fruit of the girl bursts into blood and cotton,
spatters the whole house as she goes,
waters the rose,
feeds the dove
so bird and flower may migrate
in search of their exact dimension.
The first seed announces the spring.

Not for me:
I inhabit a desert of turbinated sugars.
Through the mulatez of the honey-colored syrup
I survey a body:
I take delight
in the unpublished canefield of the pubis,
in the plumes of feathers on the head,
in the shavings of the underarms,
in the small sugarmill of the breasts,
in the thick legs,
in the bronze bowl of the bellybutton,
in the centrifuge of the eyes,
in the refined teeth.

I know only how to listen to my own blood
and the anguish
before the inevitable beauty of the mother-of-pearl and
turquoise child,
the figurine
before whom open-mouthed I stretch my hand

alguien que me condena a la caricia
                              y a quien la burla empuja
a encerrarse en cualquier agujero,
                    cucurucho,
                    barquillo helado
o escondite donde la muerte empolle sus huevos.

Y allá voy
arrastando un cuerpo
                    que no me pertenece,
haciendo mío
un miedo
          que no me corresponde,
aceptando
una fealdad
que no engendro.
Y
    allí
      estoy
rompiendo el lago de azogue que no aprendió el mito de Narciso.
Inventándome la perpetuidad del Eco.

El dedo lento traza el círculo de mi eternidad:
siete letras:
                mi nombre de decir que sí,
                mi nombre de llenar el espacio,
                mi nombre-palabra,
                mi nombre-poema.
El verbo que reorganiza el caos. La profecía que ordena.
Sólo en la madurez el fruto se hace humilde y besa la tierra.
Búscate una leyenda y que en ella se unan quien no soy
y quien serás ya para siempre.
Pífanos y caramillos en el secreto del Monte, en la joroba del
    yerbero.
Toca la flauta y acompáñate
                    como los duendes
con el silbo que despierta a la yagruma o a la anémona.
Siéntate en la copa de la ceiba.

someone who condemns me to a caress
                              and whom mockery pushes
to hide herself in any small hole,
                        paper cone,
                        ice-cream cone
or secret place where death hatches her eggs.

And I go there
dragging a body
            that doesn't belong to me,
making
a fear
        that is mine but not my own,
accepting
an ugliness
I don't give birth to.
And
   there
        I am
breaking the quicksilver lake that didn't learn the myth of Narcissus.
Inventing for myself the perpetuity of Echo.

The slow finger traces the circle of my eternity:
seven letters:
                my name to say yes,
                my name to fill the space,
                my word-name,
                my poem-name.
The verb that reorganizes chaos. The prophesy that determines.
Only in maturity does the fruit grow humble and kiss the earth.
Look for a legend and in it let who I am not
and who you will be always unite.
Fifes and woodpipes in the secret of the Sacred Wild, and in
the herb collector's hump.
Play the flute, accompany yourself
                        like the elves
whose whistle wakes the trumpetwood or the anemones.
Sit down in the crown of the ceiba.

Dilúyete en el girasol o en un príncipe negro.
Véngate en la compasión del flamboyán.
Sopla indiferente,
sopla traviesa,
sopla ingenua
ahora que tienes para ti sola la demencia de las palabras,
el pájaro de fuego y cristal de la sabiduría.
Sopla hasta el punto anterior al estallido
ahora que la isla es una hoguera.

Quizá fue antes o después:
el tiempo es un saltimbanqui
                              sin trapecio
al que asirse,
                              ni red
que le permita repetir la cabriola, propia o ajena.
¿Qué importa que la carpa se deshaga?
¿Qué importa el destino de las fieras?
Es el tiempo,
                todo el tiempo,
quien ahora se columpia y arriesga.
Detenlo ahí.
              Retrátalo
cuando aún es la flexibilidad y la gracia del reto.

Un pregón abre las ventanas:
                    un policía y un chivato las cierran.
Oculto en el aroma del lechón y los remordimientos
esplende el pino en la cocina.
                              En la cocina
adoban con mojo criollo las tradiciones.
                                        Manzanilla y buen jerez
nunca faltan en la cocina.
                              En la cocina
la sagrada familia y los reyes del oriente.

Dilute yourself in the sunflower or in a príncipe negro.
Avenge yourself in the compassion of the flamboyán.
Blow indifferently,
blow mischievously,
blow candidly
now that you have for yourself alone the dementia of words,
the firebird and crystal of wisdom.
Blow to point of explosion
now that the island is a bonfire.

Perhaps it was before or after:
Time is an acrobat
                    without a trapeze
to grasp,
                        nor a net
to let him repeat the nimble leap, his own or another's.
What does it matter if the tent disintegrates?
What does it matter the fate of wild beasts?
It is time,
        all of time,
that now swings and takes risks.
Stop it there.
            Take a picture
while there is still the flexibility and grace of the challenge yet
    in the air.

A vendor's cry opens the windows:
                        a policeman and an informer close them.
Hidden in the aroma of suckling pig and remorse
shines the pine wood in the kitchen.
                        In the kitchen
traditions soak in creole marinade.
                        Chamomile and good sherry
are never lacking in the kitchen.
                        In the kitchen
the sacred family and the kings from the east.

                                                    En la cocina
                        la vianda hervida,
                        el congrí,
                        la gallina de guinea,
                        el pavo plebeyo,
                        los dátiles babilónicos,
                        las nueces y avellanas,
                        los higos,
                        el turrón de almendra o yema.
Prestidigitación invernal de la burguesía:
                                                    magia negra
de esconder en la manga
                        o
                        en la cocina
el hámago de la isla.
Como si la isla fuera un pañuelo amarillo para que la escondieran.

                        Ay,
                        toca las maracas
                        mulatón,
                        que me muero
                        por tu son.

                        Ay,
                        toca la maracas
                        y el bongó,
                        que mi Cuba
                        es un fiestón.

Pero la Isla camina sobre el llanto.
La Isla ayuna en el monte de las guayabas.
La Isla se crucifica sobre los huesos de sus muertos.
Ya no hay tango,
                        novela,
                        bolero,
                        ¡vida! más triste que el palpitar del torturado.
Ni navaja más filosa que el metal de una sirena.
De pronto
las muchachas decidieron no morirse de amor o de anemia.

                                        In the kitchen
                    the boiled roots,
                    the congrí,
                    the Guinea hen,
                    the ordinary turkey,
                    the Babylonian dates,
                    the walnuts and hazelnuts,
                    the figs,
                    the almond nougat or eggnog bars.
The winter prestidigitation of the bourgeois:
                                        black magic
to hide up one's sleeve
                    or
                    in the kitchen
the island's bee glue.
As if the island were a yellow handkerchief so that she could be hidden.

                    Ay,
                    play the maracas
                    mulatto,
                    I'm dying
                    for your beat.

                    Ay,
                    play the maracas
                    and the bongo drums,
                    my Cuba
                    is a festival.

But the Island walks on tears.
The Island fasts on the mount of guavas.
The Island crucifies herself on the bones of her dead.
There is no more tango,
                    novel,
                    bolero,
                    Life! Sadder than the tremors of the tortured.
No razorblade sharper than the siren's metal.
Suddenly
girls decide not to die of love or of anemia:

Por las calles desfilan como banderas.
Tras el tremolar de sus faldas la ciudad enmudece
        victrola
        y tambor.
        Guaguancó
        y chancleta.
De rojo y negro van las muchachas al encuentro de sus parejas.
En la sombra,
y el polvo,
y el silencio,
           se oficia las nupcias de esta época.
Salen entonces de viaje. Sobre una llaga navegan:
Barqueros de sangre y pus
             tienen por remo una estrella.
Nunca duermen. Siempre bogan:
En la otra orilla espera la ceniza,
                fiel barbecho
de sus sueños.
                       Zafra del fuego,
serena señal
        sobre sus frentes abiertas.

Intramuros del horror en casa han levantado una atalaya:
peldaño a peldaño del jadeo
        subo hasta la lluvia.
Veo mi nombre naciendo
        en río salvaje,
        en trino,
        en cielo.
Mi nombre de verde
        bosque.
Y de Llano. Y de Sierra.
Pero la lluvia cierra su párpado:
Abril devuelve el silencio a las aceras.
La casa es la trinchera del miedo:
             Ya no hablamos ni en voz baja:
Nos hemos convertido en velones de cera.
Soy una niña a la que todos niegan
        usar de un nombre que huele a pólvora y cólera.

On the streets they march like flags.
Behind the waving of their skirts the city becomes a mute
                    victrola
                    and drum.
                    Guaguancó
                    and chancleta.
Dressed in red and black go the girls to meet their partners.
In the shade,
and the dust,
and the silence,
                    the nuptials of this time are celebrated.
Then they go on a trip. They sail on an open sore:
Boatmen of blood and pus
                    have a star for a paddle.
They never sleep. They always row:
On the other shore await the ashes,
                                    faithful fallow
of their dreams.
                                    Sugar harvest of fire,
serene sign
            on their open foreheads.

Walled-up in the horror at home they have raised a lookout tower:
stair by stair panting
                    I mount up to the rain.
I see my name being born
                    in the wild river,
                    in the bird song,
                    in the sky.
My name of green
                woods.
And of the Llano. And of the Sierra.
But the rain closes its eyelids:
April returns silence to the sidewalks.
The house is the trench of fear:
                    Now we don't speak even in a whisper:
We have become wax candles.
I am a girl to whom all deny
            a name that smells like gunpowder and cholera.

Soy una niña exiliada en el día de la espera.

Pero eso ocurrió antes
de que el arriero perdiera la mansedumbre
de la bestia.
      Antes
de que los horcones mostraran su gangrena.
      Antes
del júbilo y la victoria.
      Antes
        del clarín y la fiesta.

La ciudad es una mariposa. La isla, delicada jardinera.
Una flor de alambre y ayes
         liba el miedo de mi parentela:
Todos quieren que adorne con sus púas
          la cintura de mi adolescencia.
Pero,
   apártense
   que voy de pluma.
   Pero,
   apártense
   que voy de prisa y vuelo
   con un fusil amoroso entre las manos
         colmenando la miel que llevo dentro.
Sólo tú,
   Ana Excilia,
        comprendes mis campanas,
campanera tú misma sin saberlo.
Sólo la madre de mi padre se asoma al balcón de sus recuerdos:

Bajo él pasa la sombra de un tranvía de silencio:
Un sombrero de pajilla está esperándola lejos:
  Aquel muchacho muerto en la violencia
que se encelaba de su taconeo.
Niña mía sin letras ni palotes
         lazarilla de un padre ciego;
muchachita de los túnicos planchados

I am an exiled girl in the day of expectation.

But that happened before
                    the muleteer lost the gentleness
of the beast.
          Before
the tree props showed their gangrene.
          Before
the jubilee and the victory.
          Before
                    the bugle and the fiesta.

The city is a butterfly. The island, a delicate gardener.
A flower of wire and sighs
                    sips my kinfolk's fear:
They all want me to adorn with their thorns
                              the waist of my adolescence.
But,
        stand aside
        I'm going with my pen.
        But,
        stand aside
        for I'm in a hurry and I fly
        with a loving rifle in my hand
                    beehiving the honey that I carry inside.
Only you,
          Ana Excilia,
                    understand my bells,
bellringer as you are without knowing it.
Only the mother of my father standing on the balcony of her
    memories:

Beneath it, the shadow of a streetcar of silence goes by:
  A straw hat is waiting for her from afar:
That boy dead in violence
who became jealous of her heel stomping.
Girl of mine without letters or a pen's downstroke,
                              lazarilla of a blind father;
little girl of ironed dresses

negociada como pieza entre negreros;
Ana Excilia Bregante, criollera,
¿cómo fue que me dijiste tu secreto?
La falsedad del anillo en tu mano,
el regazo abandonado y desierto.
Ana Excilia
    del pan recién horneado,
        nuestro sin que sea nuestro:
Ana Excilia
    de los **haigas** y los pájaros,
      de los aparecidos y los cuentos;
Ana Excilia
    de las pulseras;
Ana Excilia mía que estás en lo incierto,
¿qué otra corona has ceñido,
      hija de mulata y de isleño,
sino la ola perfumada
    de la playa de tu pelo?
Y tu cetro, ¿qué lo enjoya,
     sino la elegancia del ají,
la altivez de la cebolla,
      la nobleza del mastuerzo?
¿Qué ejército ha cuidado,
    Ana Excilia,
de tu reino,
    sino el corazón de roja grana
acantonado en medio de mi pecho?
Ana Excilia Bregante,
    Seña Cuca,
voy a celebrar tu nombre
      en unas manos
renegridas del carbón,
    blanqueadas por la lejía,
      amarillentas de resebo.
Píntate los labios,
    Ana Excilia
ponte tus peinetas,
    el collar de perlas falsas,

    traded like an object among slave traders;
Ana Excilia Bregante, criollera,
how was it that you told me your secret?
The falsehood of the ring on your finger,
the abandoned lap, deserted lap.
Ana Excilia
   of the recently baked bread,
       ours though not ours;
Ana Excilia
   of the **ain'ts** and the birds,
     of the ghosts and the stories;
Ana Excilia
   of the bracelets;
my Ana Excilia who art in uncertainty,
what other crown have you fitted,
     daughter of mulatta and Canary Islander,
if not the perfumed wave
    of the beach of your hair?
And your scepter, who jewels it,
     if not the elegance of the green pepper,
the arrogance of the onion,
     the nobility of the watercress?
What army has guarded,
    Ana Excilia,
your kingdom,
   but the heart of scarlet grain
billeted at the center of my breast?
Ana Excilia Bregante,
    Seña Cuca,
I'm going to celebrate your name
     with worker's hands
blackened again by coal,
    whitened by bleach,
     stained by yellow mortar.
Paint your lips,
   Ana Excilia,
put on your hair combs,
    your necklace of false pearls,

el vestido de bodas
                y retretas.
Saca el pericón de sándalo,
                        desempólvalo de quejas.
Y abanícame la ciudad,
                que no detenga su danza
                            de giralda coqueta:
Ven conmigo a compartir el amor
                            y amamantar a la Primavera.
Ana Excilia Bregante,
                ahora,
                        niega esta casa,
                    niega la usura del bolso y la fiambrera.
Niégame el nombre
                si con él no alcanzo la totalidad de la entrega.
Ana Excilia Bregante,
                ahora,
                y no en la hora de tu muerte:
                        Me tocó perder.
                            Pero
                sálvame para cuando en ti vaya
                o para cuando a mí vengas.
                                Te espero
                con la cama tendida
                    olorosa a vetiver y menta,
                con la leche ahumada,
                    con mis manos y mis polichinelas.
                Excilia,
                    tú,
                        siempre Excilia:
                        nombre de mi nombre:
                        nieta,
                        guardiana:
                        compañera.

Yo no soy la heredera del desconcierto.
Desterraron mi nombre y me desterraron.

your wedding gown
    and sound the retreat.
Take out the large sandalwood fan,
      dust off its complaints.
And fan the city for me,
    let it not stop its dance
       like a fickle weathervane:
Come with me to share love
     and to suckle Springtime.
Ana Excilia Bregante,
    now,
      deny this house,
    deny the profits of the purse and pantry.
Deny me my name
    if with it I don't reach the fullness of surrender.
Ana Excilia Bregante,
    now,
     and not at the hour of your death:
      It was my turn to lose.
       But
     save me for when I go in you
     or for when you come to me.
       I'll wait for you
    with the bed made
     odorous of vetiver grass and mint,
    with steamed milk
   with my lullabies and my punchinello.
    Excilia,
     you,
      always Excilia:
      name of my name:
      grandchild,
      guardian,
      compañera.

I am not the inheritor of bewilderment.
They banished my name and they banished me.

Me condenaron a llevarlo
                    de puerta
                    en
                    puerta
siendo la que se fue o a la que han ido.
Insomne de mi cama, ayuna de mi mesa.
La casa ya no existe:
                    nadie la vela;
en el vórtice del ciclón
sólo se admite al que tenga vocación de ventolera:
Libre estoy en el espacio
                    de la libertad primera
para encontrarme el origen
                    en el hijo que me engendra.

La mata de orégano perfuma humilde
                        la mano que la quiebra.
Un niño ríe y me alarga la hoja.
Y la huelo.
            Y se la doy a oler.
                        Y ríe.
Tengo el vientre de pájaro
                porque me he dado al mundo
en la alegría de la tierra.
Crece rápido,
            pecho de mi hijo;
endurécete,
            mano de mi hijo;
ponte fuerte,
            espalda de mi hijo;
elévate ya,
            estatura de mi hijo;
                            mi nombre te espera.

Pero no el pequeño y extraño nombre
de los papeles oficiales.
Ese talismán fuera de moda,
                esa vieja contraseña,

They condemned me to bear it
                    from door
                    to
                    door
being the one who left or the one who also was left.
Insomniac of my bed, keeper of the fast at my table.
The house no longer exists:
                    nobody watches over it;
in the vortex of the cyclone
only those with a vocation for gusts of wind are admitted:
I am free within the space
                    of the first freedom
to encounter my origin
                    in the son who engenders me.

The oregano plant humbly perfumes
                    the hand of the one who breaks it.
A child laughs and he hands me the leaf.
And I smell it.
            And I give it for him to smell.
                        And he laughs.
I have a womb of birds
            because I've given myself to the world
in the joy of the earth.
Grow quickly,
            breast of my son;
harden,
        hand of my son;
get strong,
        back of my son;
rise up at once,
            height of my son;
                            my name awaits you.

But not the small and strange name
of the official papers.
That outdated talisman,
            that old countersign,

ese bastión de familia,
¿a quién importarle, sino a mí?
O a la que dicen que soy
                        por pura intuición o maledicencia.
No hablo del nombre que me dijeron
para poder hablar con las estrellas.
Para mi nombre de siete letras
                    hechas de miedo y más miedo
no quiero carteles ni titulares ni entrevistas ni suspiros ni ediciones ni
homenajes ni marquesinas ni saraos ni besamanos ni jubileos.
—No extraño lo que no he tenido,
            no aspiro a lo que no tengo—.
Sino para el otro:
            Mi nombre
de pie y camino,
mi nombre.
            Mi nombre
de yagua y cieno,
    mi nombre.
            Mi nombre
de grasa y humo,
    mi nombre.
            Mi nombre,
de algodón y fuego,
    mi nombre.
            Mi nombre
de alcohol y noche,
    mi nombre.
            Mi nombre
de caldera y trueno,
    mi nombre.
            Mi nombre
de río y miel,
    mi nombre.
            Mi nombre
de cueva y cielo,
    mi nombre.
            Mi nombre

that bastion of families,
to whom would it matter, but to me?
Or to the one they say I am
                              by pure intuition or slander.
I am not talking about the name they told me
so that I could speak with the stars.
For my name of seven letters
                        made of fear and more fear
I do not wish posters or headlines, interviews, sighs, editions,
homages, billboards, soirées, kiss-my-hand, jubilees.
—I do not miss what I have not had.
              I do not aspire to what I do not have—.
But for the other:
              My name
of foot and road,
my name.

> *couplets refer to yoruban deities*

              My name
of yagua and mire,
      my name.
              My name
of grease and smoke,
      my name.
              My name
of cotton and fire,
      my name.
              My name
of alcohol and night,
      my name.
              My name
of caldron and thunder,
      my name.
              My name
of river and honey,
      my name.
              My name
of cave and sky,
      my name.
              My name

de risa abierta,
    mi nombre.
        Mi nombre
de arco y viento,
    mi nombre.
        Mi nombre
de grano y llaga,
    mi nombre.
        Mi nombre
de mar y hierro,
    mi nombre.
        Mi nombre
de musgo y pétalo,
    mi nombre.
        Mi nombre
de cristal y acero,
    mi nombre.
Mi nombre
    en el nombre de los que recién deciden su nombre y
                sus recuerdos.
Mi nombre
    para precipitarlo como una lluvia sobre el cántaro de mi
                archipiélago.

of open laughter,
    my name.
        My name
of arc and wind,
    my name.
        My name
of grain and blister,
    my name.
        My name
of sea and iron,
    my name.
        My name
of moss and petal,
    my name.
        My name
of crystal and steel,
    my name.
My name
    in the name of those who've recently decided their name and
                            their memories.
My name
    to precipitate like rain on the cántaro of my
                        archipelago.

Danzón inconcluso
para Noche e Isla

Dos patrias tengo yo: Cuba y la noche.

José Martí

Para Fina y Cintio, cubanos

La Noche
goza de la isla dormida. Inocente. Frágil
como un pájaro fatigado del que sólo se sabe que vive
por el ala.
Ala insólita flotando sobre las aguas: alas de agua.
Ala que es isla.
Y es ala.

Pero un golpe de viento. Una ola. Una hoja caída
de otros mundos
la
sorprende.

Entonces,

se despereza:
el cuello estira,   levanta la cabeza coronada,
agita el plumaje poderoso,
se eleva.
Rompe la jaula de la noche.
Se eleva.
Rompe el espacio de la noche.
Se eleva.
Rompe el vacío de la noche.
Se eleva.

Le nace en el pecho un canto de despaciosa anchura,
una serenidad de azul. Una lámpara suave y diamantina.
Y busca en su vuelo nupcial otro trino,
el que antes fue noche y luego, jaula y después, espacio y
más tarde, vacío.

Unfinished Danzón
for Night and Island

> I have two homelands: Cuba and the night.
>
> José Martí

For Fina and Cintio, Cubans.

                    Night
enjoys the sleeping Island. Innocent. Fragile
like a weary bird known to be living only
                    because of its wing.
Strange wing floating on the waters: wings of water.
                    Wing that is island.
                    And is wing.

But a burst of wind. A wave. A leaf fallen
                    from other worlds
                    surprises
                    it.

Then,

            it drowses:
its neck stretches,   raises its crowned head,
                    shakes its powerful plumage,
                    and rises.
Breaks the cage of night.
                    And rises.
Breaks the space of night.
                    And rises.
Breaks the void of night.
                    And rises.

A song of slow expanse is born in its breast,
a serenity of blue. A lamp soft and like a diamond.
And in its nuptial flight it looks for another trill,
a prior trill that was first night and then, cage and then, place and
later, void.

Y ahora es ave

en celo

y

esperando.

Isla y Noche, una.

Libres

de la inmensidad y la fijeza. Consagradas
en el instante escapado en que el ave se transmuta
en flor y en rocío.
Lo eterno sobre lo infinito. Libándose.

Después

el éxtasis.

Después

el secreteo íntimo de los dones.

Después

el vértigo del ahora que ya es memoria.
(Ah, el corazón oculto donde el pico de la Isla escarba el latido
misterioso de la Noche.)
*Pero ya no es lo que fue, sino el anillo prodigando su imagen en
el tiempo. No la línea, sino el círculo despojado de su pulpa. El
rumor oval del fuego en el árbol, en el madero y en la ceniza. El
juego errabundo de las mutaciones.*

La Noche flota dormida sobre las aguas
—fatigada cual pájaro inocente del que mucho se ignora
que no muere
y por el ala.
La Isla gozosa la mira.

Una constelación nonata se encorala en los arrecifes.
Un rechinar de carretas retumba de estrella en estrella.

Soy la Noche   Soy la Isla.

Dos patrias en mí que las contengo.

90 en mayo

And now it is bird
in heat
and
in expectation.

Island and Night, one.
                Free
from immensity and fixedness. Consecrated
in the fleeing instant when the bird transforms itself
                into flower and dew.
Eternity above infinity. Sipping itself.
Then
        ecstasy.
Then
        the intimate gossiping of gifts,
Then
        the vertigo of the now that is already memory.
(Oh, the hidden heart where the Island's beak scratches the mys-
    terious beat of the Night.)
It is no longer what it was, but rather a ring lavishing its image
in time. It is not the line, but rather the circle despoiled of its
flesh. The oval murmur of fire in the tree, in the log and in the
ashes. The wandering game of mutations.

Night floats sleeping on the waters
—weary like an innocent bird about which much is ignored
                that does not die
                        because of its wing.
The joyful Island watches her.

An unborn constellation encorals itself in the reefs.
A grating of wagons resounds from star to star.

I am the Night.   I am the island.

Two homelands contained in me.

                        May 1990

Epílogo

Es mucho la muerte cuando puede con un trueno humano semejante. Y mucho la vida cuando puede con una muerte de tanto empuje, bufido y señorío. Excilia Saldaña ha muerto de su muerte natural que es la de la ceiba, capitana de cien brazos como la llamara Gabriela, derribada por el huracán del asma. Un asma enfurecida de amor por ella porque le circulaba en las venas el oxígeno incandescente de la mulatez mayor. Le escribió un ovillejo a Maceo. Maceísta era, fundadora de la escuela maceísta de nuestra poesía, única maestra, que sepamos, de ella, madraza de la lírica épica para grandes y chicos, chiqueadora de la grandeza y familiona de todas las sazones, girasoles, y yerbas aromáticas. Su poema fue su nombre; su parnaso, su familia; ronca llegaba y ronca se iba, mirando con el ojo virado lo que ningún otro veía, bellísima habanera andaluza de la época de los astilleros de los que salió, astilla cristalina, la clave de granadillo, sin olvidar los cueros. Qué mujer, Dios mío, qué chorro de poesía, qué ternura desafiante, qué tronco de coraje y sabiduría ornada de collares, qué cuajarones de conversación y ahogada risa, trayéndonos albahaca y versos y un hilo de nylon irrompible para la tendedera. Ahí cuelgan ahora nuestras telas y entretelas recordándola siempre. Porque ella sí está muerta de verdad como antes estuvo viva. Porque su única vida sigue siendo la verdad.[1]

Cintio Vitier

27 de octubre de 1999

Afterword

Death is too great when it overpowers such overwhelming human thunder. And life too great when it overpowers a death of such thrust, force of wind, and dominion. Excilia Saldaña has died her natural death, which is that of the ceiba (captain of a hundred arms as Gabriela would call it), fallen by the hurricane of her asthma. A furious asthma in love with her because in her veins circulated the incandescent oxygen of the great mulatez. She composed a rondeau to Maceo. A Maceo aficionado was she, founder of the Maceo school of poetry, singular teacher, as far as we know, of that Maceo school; doting mother of the lyrical epic for adults and children; asking for caresses from greatness, and family matron of all flavors, sunflowers and aromatic herbs. Her poem was her name, her Parnassus, her family; hoarse she would arrive and hoarse she would leave, seeing with her veering eye what no one else saw; a beautiful Andalusian woman from Havana, of the time of the shipyards, from which she came, crystalline splinter, mystery of the tamarind, without forgetting the lashes. What a woman, my God, what gushing of poetry, what defying tenderness, what core of courage and wisdom-garlanded necklaces, what clots of conversation and muffled laughter, bringing us sweet basil and verses and an unbreakable nylon thread for our clothesline. There, our clothes and our interlinings hang to remember her always. Because she is truly dead as before she was alive. Because her unique life continues to be the truth.[1]

Cintio Vitier

October 27, 1999

Glossary

apetedbí—woman, wife of Orula, the orisha of divination; assistant to the babalawo, Afro-Cuban priest.

batá—Afro-Cuban lead drum, known as Iyá or the mother drum.

brisca—Spanish card game.

cántaro—basin; also used to connote hard rains: "llueve a cántaros."

Carabalí—person from the Calabar region in West Africa; refers to a slave purported to be of a rebellious nature.

ceiba—silk-cotton tree endemic to Cuba. Revered by Afro-Cubans as the temple of their deities.

chancleta—wooden sandal.

compañera—comrade.

congrí—black beans and white rice.

criollera—slave who served as wet-nurse to Cuban babies, black and white.

ebbó—ritual cleansing used as an offering in Afro-Cuban ceremonies.

flamboyán—flamboyan tree, royal poinciana.

galán de noche—night jessamine; suitor of the night.

guaguancó—Afro-Cuban popular dance that originated as a ritual dance.

guayabera—elegant pleated tropical shirt.

güije—gnome: a mythical black child who inhabits puddles and lakes in Afro-Cuban cultures.

hipsipilas—chrysalis of owlet moths.

Iyá—Afro-Cuban lead drum. In the Carabalí language, fish, mother, foundation.

jutía—rat-like rodent.

lazarilla—female caretaker/companion to blind person, from the Spanish picaresque novel *Lazarillo de Tormes*.

Llano—the plains, signifying here the revolutionary struggle in the city.

mulatez—racial mixing; cultural integration of European and African practices.

omiero—mix of blessed waters with herbs, ashes, blood, etc., used in Afro-Cuban rituals of cleansing and healing.

otá—divining stone.

príncipe negro—red rose; black prince.

Sierra—Sierra Maestra, site of the guerrilla revolution during the 1950s.

yagua—top leaves from the palm tree used in roof building.

Notes

Introduction

1. *Juventude Rebelde,* July 21, 1999, 2. My translation.
2. Ramírez Enríquez, "El vientre del pez," *Revista Extramuros* 5 (Jan. 2001): 26. My translation.
3. See Bibliography for essays written by Davies.
4. Saldaña, *Afro-Hispanic Review,* Fall 2000, 8–11. My translation.
5. Saldaña, *La Noche,* book cover autobiography. My translation.
6. Saldaña, "*Monólogo de la Esposa,*" 86–100.
7. Lydia Cabrera, *El Monte.* Miami: Collección del Chicherekú, 1992.
8. For a thorough study of literary allusions in this poem, see Catherine Davies, "Mother Africa and Cultural Memory," *A Place in the Sun?* 188–94.
9. Saldaña, *Mi Nombre (Antielegía familiar),* 1991.

The Wife's Monologue

1. Butterflies—refers to the Cuban national flower, *Hedychium coronarium.*
2. Lyrics from a tango.

Afterword

1. Cintio Vitier, *La Isla Infinita,* July–December 1999, 33. Translated by Flora González Mandri and Rosamond Rosenmeier.

Bibliography

Abudu, Gabriel A. "African Oral Arts in Excilia Saldaña's *Kele Kele*." *Afro-Hispanic Review* 19.2 (Fall 2000): 21–29.

Davies, Catherine. "Cross-Cultural Homebodies in Cuba: The Poetry of Excilia Saldaña." In *Latin American Women's Writing: Feminist Readings in Theory and Crisis*, ed. Anny Brooksbanck Jones and Catherine Davies, 179–200. Oxford: Clarendon Press, 1996.

———. "Mother Africa and Cultural Memory: Nancy Morejón, Georgina Herrera, Excilia Saldaña." In *A Place in the Sun?: Women Writers in Twentieth-Century Cuba*, 165–95. London and New Jersey: Zed Books, 1997.

———. "Women Writers in Twentieth Century Cuba: An Eight-Point Survey." In *Framing the Word: Gender and Genre in Caribbean Women's Writing*, ed. Joan Anim-Adds, 138–58. London: Whiting & Birch, 1996.

———. "Hybrid Texts: Family, State, and Empire in a Poem by Black Cuban Poet Excilia Saldaña." In *Comparing Postcolonial Literatures: Dislocations*, ed. Ashok Bery and Patricia Murray. New York: St. Martin's Press, 1999.

García Marruz, Fina. "Sobre *Mi Nombre*" (About *My Name*). *Revista Casa de las Américas* 150 (1985): 173.

García Marruz, Fina, Félix Pita Rodríguez, and Cintio Vitier. "Reviews of *Kele Kele* and *Mi Nombre*." *Afro-Hispanic Review* 19.2 (Fall 2000): 12–13.

González, Flora M. "El afán de nombrarse en la obra poética de Excilia Saldaña" (The zeal of naming herself in the poetic works of Excilia Saldaña). *Afro-Hispanic Review* 16.2 (Fall 1997): 34–42.

———. "De la tradición épico-lírica a la yoruba en *Kele Kele* de Excilia Saldaña" (From the epic-lyric to the Yoruba tradition in *Kele Kele* by Excilia Saldaña). *Actas del Congreso Beresit II*, 171–77. Toledo: Cofradía Internacional de Investigadores, 1992.

———. "Excilia Saldaña, In Memoriam 1946–1999." *Afro-Hispanic Review* 19.2 (Fall 2000): 3–7.

James, Conrad. "Women, Life-writing, and National Identity in Cuba: Excilia Saldaña's *Mi nombre: Antielegía familiar*." In *The Cultures of the Hispanic Car-*

ibbean, ed. Conrad James and John Perivolaris, 50–71. Gainesville: University Press of Florida, 2000.

Pita Rodríguez, Félix. "Una carta sobre *Kele Kele*" (A letter about *Kele Kele*). *Caimán Barbudo* (July 1989): 20.

Saldaña, Excilia. "Autobiografía" (Autobiography). *Breaking the Silences: An Anthology of 20th-Century Poetry by Cuban Women,* trans. Margaret Randall, 200, 202. Vancouver: Pulp Press, 1982.

———. "A través del espejo" (Through the looking glass). *Letras Cubanas* 15 (July–December 1989): 41–42.

———. *Bulgaria, el país de las rosas* (Bulgaria, the country of roses). Havana: Editorial Gente Nueva, 1987.

———. *Cantos para Mayito y una paloma* (Songs for Mayito and a dove). Havana: Editorial Unión, 1984.

———. *Cantos para Mayito y una paloma* (Songs for Mayito and a dove). Buenos Aires: Ediciones El Hacedor, forthcoming.

———. *Cine de horror y misterio: Ensayo* (Films of horror and mystery: an essay). Havana: Universidad de La Habana, 1978.

———. *Compay Tito* (My buddy Tito). Havana: Editorial Gente Nueva, 1988.

———. "Lo cotidiano trascendente: Reflexiones sobre mi obra poética" (The transcendent quotidian: reflections on my poetic work). *Afro-Hispanic Review* 19.2 (Fall 2000): 8–11.

———. "Danzón inconcluso para Noche e Isla" (Unfinished danzón for night and island). *Letras Cubanas* 18 (n.d.): 161–64.

———. *De la isla del tesoro a la isla de la juventud* (From treasure island to the isle of youth). Havana: Editorial Gente Nueva, 1988.

———. *10 Poetas de la Revolución* (10 poets of the revolution). Havana: Universidad de La Habana, 1974.

———. *Flor para amar* (A flower to love). Havana: Editorial Gente Nueva, 1980.

———. *Jícara de miel: El libro de todas mis nanas* (Honey gourd: the book of all my lullabies). Havana: Editorial Gente Nueva, 2000.

———. *Kele Kele.* Havana: Editorial Letras Cubanas, 1987.

———. *Mi Nombre (Antielegía Familiar)* (My name [a family anti-elegy]). Havana: Ediciones Unión, 1991.

———. *El misterioso caso de los maravillosos cascos de Doña Cuca Bregante* (The mysterious case of the marvelous guava shells of Mam Cuca Bregante). Havana: Editorial Capitán San Luis, 1992.

———. *La Noche* (Night). Havana: Editorial Gente Nueva, 1989.

———. *Poesía de amor y de combate* (Poems of love and combat). Havana: Editorial Gente Nueva, 1981.

———. *La pupila inquieta* (The restive pupil). Havana: Editorial Unión, forthcoming.

———. *El refranero de La Víbora* (Collection of refrains from La Víbora). Havana: Editorial Letras Cubanas, 1989.

———. *Soñando y viajando* (Dreaming and traveling). Havana: Editorial Gente Nueva, 1980.

———. *Un testigo de la historia* (A witness of history). Havana: Editorial Gente Nueva, 1978.

———. "Tríptico de los contrasonetos anacrónicos" (Tryptich of anachronic counter sonnets). *Afro-Hispanic Review* 19.2 (Fall 2000): 14.

———. "Vieja Trova sobre soporte CD ROM" (An old love ballad in support of CD-ROM). (Fragments). *Afro-Hispanic Review* 19.2 (Fall 2000): 15–20.

———. "Vieja Trova sobre soporte CD ROM" (An old love ballad in support of CD-ROM). *Isla Infinita* 1.2 (July–December, 1999): 22–33.

———. "Deus" (God). *Lovers and Comrades*, ed. Amanda Hopkinson, 121. London: The Women's Press. 1989.

———. "From My Name (A Family Anti-Elegy)," eds. Ruth Behar and Juan León. *Michigan Quarterly Review* 33.3 (Summer 1994): 543–47.

———. "From My Name (A Family Anti-Elegy)." *Bridges to Cuba / Puentes a Cuba: Cuban and Cuban-American artists, writers, and scholars explore identity, nationality and homeland*, ed. Ruth Behar, 184–88. Ann Arbor: The University of Michigan Press, 1995.

———. "Ofumeli." *Afro-Cuba*, eds. Pedro Pérez Sarduy and Jean Stubbs, 163–68. Brooklyn: Ocean Press, 1993.

Ramírez Enríquez, Consuelo. "El vientre del pez." *Revista Extramuros* 5 (January 2001): 26.

Santos Moray, Mercedes. *Juventud Rebelde*, 21 July 1999, 2.

Vitier, Cintio. "Es mucho la muerte . . ." *La Isla Infinita* 1.2 (July–December 1999): 33.

Flora González Mandri, Cuban-born, associate professor of writing, literature, and publishing at Emerson College in Boston, is presently working on a volume of critical essays titled *Braiding the Tresses of Memory: Autobiography and National Identity by Afro-Cuban Women*.

Rosamond Rosenmeier is a poet, critic, and professor emerita at the University of Massachusetts, Boston. Her publications include the critical study *Anne Bradstreet Revisited*, and the collection of poems *Lines Out*.

Excilia Saldaña (1946–1999) was a Cuban poet, essayist, translator, and editor of poetry and fiction for children.

Alexis Esquivel is a Cuban, Havana-based artist whose works have been exhibited and collected in Cuba, the United States, Canada, Italy, Brazil, Spain, and Mexico.

Nancy Morejón is a Cuban poet, translator, cultural critic, and member of Casa de las Américas and the Royal Academy of Cuban Language.

Cintio Vitier is a distinguished Cuban poet, literary critic, editor, novelist, and member of the poetry group Orígenes.